STUDY GUIDE
ROBERT E. NUNLEY

THE CULTURAL LANDSCAPE

AN INTRODUCTION TO
HUMAN GEOGRAPHY
Fifth Edition

JAMES M. RUBENSTEIN

Severin M. Roberts, M.A.
University of Kansas

W. Lanham Lister, M.A.
University of Kansas

PRENTICE HALL, UPPER SADDLE RIVER, NJ 07458

Production Editor: *James Buckley*
Production Supervisor: *Joan Eurell*
Acquisitions Editor: *Wendy Rivers*
Production Coordinator: *Alan Fischer*

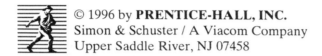 © 1996 by **PRENTICE-HALL, INC.**
Simon & Schuster / A Viacom Company
Upper Saddle River, NJ 07458

Printed in the United States of America

10 9 8 7 6 5 4 3 2 1

ISBN 0-13-459504-1

Prentice-Hall International (UK) Limited, *London*
Prentice-Hall of Australia Pty. Limited, *Sydney*
Prentice-Hall Canada, Inc., *Toronto*
Prentice-Hall Hispanoamericana, S.A., *Mexico*
Prentice-Hall of India Private Limited, *New Delhi*
Prentice-Hall of Japan, Inc., *Tokyo*
Simon & Schuster Asia Pte. Ltd., *Singapore*
Editora Prentice-Hall do Brasil, Ltda., *Rio de Janeiro*

Contents

Preface

The present study guide was produced by the three authors, aided by many students from the Geography Department of the University of Kansas. Mr. Lister prepared the early drafts of most of the material. Ms. Roberts prepared the early drafts of two chapters and an intermediate draft of the others. Dr. Nunley designed and critiqued all drafts, prepared the final draft; and assumes full responsibility for any errors or shortcomings. Hyper-media (and other electronic versions) are under development. Comments and suggestions are welcome. E-mail: (nunley@ukans.edu).

CHAPTER ONE

BASIC CONCEPTS

OVERVIEW

Chapter One details the building blocks of human geography and gives explanations of each block. The historical roots of geography, as they were developed by scholars of past times, are set forth. The *"Where"* of geography is portrayed by the four techniques employed to locate sites on the Earth's surface. Included among these techniques are the concepts of latitude and longitude which measure accurately the location of any point on the surface of the Earth. A brief history of geography is then presented. The *"Why"* of geography is defined in terms of Regional Analysis and Spatial Analysis, each of which is expanded greatly in this chapter. Types of regions and patterns of distribution are summarized. An introduction to physical processes and climate types is offered. The end of Chapter One gives two examples of places which have been altered by human actions; one project was successful, and one was not.

SELECTED NOTES

Definition of Geography (3-5): Some people believe that geography is memorizing capitals and countries, climates and crop types, as well as other facts that may initially appear "trivial." Geography is much more, for it combines areal information, and intertwines it in such a way as to give a better understanding of the traits of places, and how those traits influence other locations around the globe. *Geography* is the scientific study of the location of people and activities around the Earth, and the reasons for their distribution. Geographers ask "**Where**" things are, "**Why**" they are there, and "**Why**" their geographic arrangements are significant. It is the scientific study of the reasons why people and things are arranged in a particular way. As historians study the logical sequence of human activities through time, geographers study the logical arrangement of human activities through space.

Components of Geography (5): *Geography* may be divided into two primary components: *1-Human Geography* and *2-Physical Geography*. *Human Geography* is the focus of this textbook, and can further be refined into three parts: *a) Cultural, b) Social,* and *c) Economic*. *Physical Geography* is often divided into *a) Climate, b) Landforms,* and *c) Vegetation*. Although this book focuses on Human Geography, human populations are directly affected by the physical environment in which they live. For example, in Somalia hunger and food deprivation have overwhelmed much of the populace. However, no single geographic variable can account for the hunger problem. Geographers examine the relationships between population growth, drought, farming practices, environmental

1

degradation, and political unrest. Consequently, parts of the explanation for the lack of food can be traced back to Human Geography and other parts to Physical Geography. A balanced geographic analysis avoids concentrating all energy upon one part of geography, without considering to some degree the other parts of geography.

Portraying the Earth (5-8): The most useful tool used in geographic studies is the **map**. The extensive use of maps tends to distinguish geography from most other disciplines. A **map** is a graphic representation of any area (at a reduced scale), on which only selected data or locational traits are shown. Maps can show distance, direction, size, or shape, as well as a great variety of other information. Mapping is essential for understanding spatial patterns- how they occur, where they occur and why they occur, at a specific location. The science of map-making is known as **cartography**. **Scale** is an important variable in map projections, as it determines how much area and how much detail a particular map represents. Scale can be presented in one of three ways: a fraction (1/24,000) or ratio (1:24,000); a written statement such as "One inch represents one mile" or a graphic bar scale (Fig. 1.1). The scale of a **small-scale map** is represented by a fraction with a large denominator, such as 1/100,000 or greater. Such a map is able to show a large surface area, but at less detail than a large-scale map. The scale of a **large-scale map** is represented by a fraction with a small denominator, such as 1/10,000 or smaller. The large-scale map represents a small land area, but at a much higher level of detail than the small-scale map. A **projection** is a method of portraying the Earth (or any portion of it) on a flat map. There are many existing map projections, but no single projection can accurately show both **equal shape** *(a conformal map)* and **equal size** *(an equal-area or equivalent map)*. In other words, no map can simultaneously be both conformal and equivalent if it portrays more than a few square feet of area. Every map has its advantages and disadvantages but, if each is used properly, much can be gained in terms of real knowledge about a given location, and misunderstandings can be minimized. The most famous projection is the **Mercator projection**, which was created in 1569 by a Flemish geographer named **Gerardus Mercator**. This projection is mathematically adjusted to attain conformity. Parallels and meridians form a square grid on the flat projection. Distortion of shape is great at the high latitudes. Consequently, school children familiar only with world maps on this projection may be led to believe Greenland is actually as large as Africa or South America, when it is actually one fourteenth the size of Africa and one ninth the size of South America. The Mercator projection also distorts direction, but it is still very useful for navigation.

Latitude and Longitude (16-20): The Earth is a sphere with a diameter of about 12,875 km (8,000 miles) and a circumference of about 40,000 km (25,000 miles). It rotates continuously on an axis that passes through the North and South poles. Halfway between the poles lies the **equator**, which splits the Earth into the northern hemisphere and the southern hemisphere. Locations on the Earth are determined by two different measurements: latitude and longitude. **Latitude** is the angular distance measured north and south of the equator. Lines of latitude are called parallels as each line is **parallel** to the equator. **Longitude** is the angular distance measured east and west on the Earth's surface. Lines of longitude are called **meridians** and they extend from pole to pole. Meridians are parallel to each other only at the equator. Both latitude and longitude are measured in degrees, minutes, and seconds. In most places, longitude is measured starting at the *prime meridian* that traditionally passes through Greenwich, England.

Maps as a Tool (5-9): Geographers also use maps to help communicate explanations of human or physical processes. By placing information on a map, geographers can share data and analyze spatial patterns in an effective and unique way. In order to communicate a geographic meaning and avoid misunderstandings, maps need to be made well, and in such a way as to convey information competently to the map's reader. Post 1950 technology has brought forth two technological innovations in mapping–*Remote Sensing* and *Geographic Information Systems (GIS)*.

Remote Sensing and Geographic Information Systems (GIS) (8-10): The acquisition of data about the Earth's surface from a satellite orbiting the planet or from another long-distance method is known as *Remote Sensing*. Imagery produced from remote sensing may be used to evaluate water pollution, weather systems, deforestation, and many other problems. *A GIS* uses computers to extrapolate knowledge from different areal data, each type of which is placed on a separate layer (Fig. 1-2). Each layer contains a certain characteristic (such as soil type, water table depth, slope, or land cover). When operated correctly a GIS can give non-intuitive and accurate answers to questions concerning such things as pollution sources, best locations for wetlands, optimum agricultural plots, potential for erosion, or which ZIP codes contain people who would like to receive a certain type of direct mail. A *Global Positioning System (GPS)* is a piece of electronic equipment which communicates with satellites, and produces the latitudinal and longitudinal coordinates for a point within a few feet of its location. The elevation of the location is also provided with most GPS units. Data thus derived can be integrated into a GIS for better analysis of a given area.

Navigation and Geography (10): Early in human history, "geography" was synonymous with *"navigation."* For example, Mediterranean sailors charted their voyages to distant lands by noting distinctive landmarks such as rock formations and islands. Similarly, Polynesian sailors used three-dimensional *"stick charts"* made of strips of palm trees and sea shells to guide them over the far reaches of the South Pacific (Fig. 1-3).

Geography in the Ancient World (10-11): Hundreds of years before the coinage of the term "geography," the ancient Greeks were concerned with geographic phenomena. *Thales of Miletus* applied basic geometric principles to measuring land area in the 6th century B.C. Later, *Aristotle* (384-322 B.C.) demonstrated that the Earth was spherical, noting that all matter falls toward the center or core of the Earth. In 325 B.C. *Pytheas* sailed to Iceland and developed a method for measuring latitude by observing the positions of certain stars. *Hipparchus* (190-125 B.C.) developed a primitive system of latitude and longitude that is conceptually equal to our current system. *Eratosthenes* (276-195 B.C.) accurately measured the Earth's circumference to within a hundred miles. He is also the first person known to use the word geography. Additionally, Eratosthenes prepared some of the world's first known maps, and divided the Earth effectively into five climatic zones. The Roman, *Strabo* (63 B.C.-A.D. 24) extensively described the known world of his time in the seventeen-volume work, Geography. He regarded the Earth as a sphere in the center of a spherical universe. *Ptolemy*

(A.D. 100-170) wrote the eight volume Guide to Geography. In China, geography was also developed by *Phei Ssiu*, a.k.a. "the father of Chinese cartography."

The Middle Ages and The Age of Exploration (11-13): After Ptolemy, geographic thought made little significant progress for nearly a thousand years in the European theater. However, beginning in the 7th century A.D., the influence of Islam upon geographic thought was great. Muslim writers such as *Edrisi, Ibn-Batuta, and Ibn-Khaldun* wrote extensively about the lands controlled by the expanding Muslim Empire. Viking adventurers from Scandinavia did much for exploration in the late part of the first millennia A.D. In 860 they arrived in Iceland from their homelands in continental Europe. *Erik the Red* sailed to *Greenland* in 981, after being banished from Iceland. *Bjarni Herjolfsson* sailed erratically South and West of Greenland in 985 and reached *Newfoundland*, he was probably the first European to reach North or South America. In 995, *Leif Eriksson* established a settlement in Newfoundland, using the former vessel of Bjarni Herjolfsson. In 1492, *Christopher Columbus* crossed the Atlantic and set anchor near Hispanola. He died in 1506 believing he had reached Asia by using a new passage. *Vasco Nunez de Balboa* viewed the Pacific from a mountain in Panama in the year 1513. He is considered to be the first European to see the world's largest ocean. In 1522 the *Victoria* became the first ship to sail around the world. It was captained by *Ferdinand Magellan* through the Atlantic and most of the Pacific (to the *Philippines*, where he was killed in a conflict with the natives). After Magellan's death, *Juan Sebastian del Cano* piloted the Victoria for the remainder of its circumnavigation of the globe to Spain. The *Straits of Magellan* near Cape Horn at the tip of South America are named after this great explorer. Geographic thought was rekindled in the seventeenth century in Europe, inspired by the recent discoveries of the Americas to the West. The German, *Bernhardus Varenius*, wrote Geographia Generalis. It stood for more than a century as the standard treatise on modern geography.

Structuring Geography Using a Scientific Framework (13-14, 41-42): *Immanuel Kant* (1724-1804), a German philosopher, believed that geography could be classified scientifically. His belief was that "Descriptions of phenomena according to place is the science of geography." In the mid 1800's, virtually all accessible knowledge of the Earth was incorporated into a large, multi-volume work called *Cosmos*. This book was compiled by the German explorer and naturalist, *Alexander von Humboldt* (1769-1859). Von Humboldt and Professor *Karl Ritter* of the University of Berlin are considered to be the cofounders of modern geography, they also developed the *"Man"-Land* relationship theory. Additionally, these two geographers believed that the physical environment determined social development, an approach known as *Environmental Determinism*. Other prominent geographers who supported Environmental Determinism included *Friedrich Ratzel*, his student *Ellen Churchill Semple*, and *Ellsworth Huntington*. Eventually, however, Environmental Determinism was replaced as the predominant paradigm of geography with *Possibilism*, a concept generally considered to be less restrictive in its thinking as well as more open to other factors that describe human interaction with environment. Possibilism advances the idea that the environment may limit some human actions, but people have the ability to adjust to their surroundings.

4

Location: Where Something Is (14-20): **Location** is the position that something occupies (on the Earth's surface). Place name, Site, Situation, and Mathematical Location are the four ways in which geographers answer the "Where" question in regards to a thing's location on the Earth. Most places on Earth have been given names, and which are known as a *Place names or* **Toponyms** (literally, place names). The name of any state, county, or other place is its place name. A **Site** is the physical characteristics of a place. For example, places which have certain climates, soils, vegetation, latitudes, and elevations have them as their site characteristics. **Situation** is the relative location of one place in respect to another, more familiar one. To say Worcester, Mass. is about 40 miles west of Boston would be divulging Worcester's situational location. **Mathematical Location** is used to locate places with a high degree of accuracy using Longitude and Latitude. Each degree of latitude or longitude is divided into 60 minutes, and each minute into 60 seconds. Therefore 104° (degrees) 59' (minutes) 04" (seconds) West would represent a very specific meridian that would pass through poles (as all meridians do) as well as the Capitol Building of the state of Colorado. The **U.S. Land Ordinance of 1785** partitioned much of the U.S. into a system of townships and ranges to encourage settlement of the West. **Principal Meridians** and **Base Lines** were used as reference points to delineate the individual townships (Fig. 1-7). For example, the first row of townships north of a baseline is known as T1N (Township One North), likewise, the first column of townships east of the principal meridians is known as R1E (Range One East). These labels serve the same purposes as do X and Y for a mathematical or geometric chart. Each square mile is known as a section (Figure 1.8). Further, a survey township is 36 sections, 6 miles to a side (36 square miles). Further, each section is divided into quadrants (northeast, northwest, southeast, or southwest quarter) each of which consists of 160 acres (.25 square miles). "Quarters" were the plot sizes that were homesteaded by many pioneers.

Regional Analysis (20-24): An area of the Earth which is defined by one or more characteristics such as climate, agriculture, industry, religion, or language is known as a **region**. The **Regional Analysis Tradition** of geography organizes the study of Earth's peoples and environments through identification of regions and their descriptions, based upon similarities and differences and the magnitudes thereof. In Latin America most people speak an Iberian Language (Spanish or Portuguese) and are Roman Catholic, and the climates are mostly tropical or sub-tropical. Therefore the phrase, Latin America, may be a useful regional designation for that part of the Western Hemisphere generally known as "The Americas."

Formal, Functional, and Vernacular Region Types (24-26): Geographers identify three types of regions–Formal, Functional, and Vernacular. A **Formal Region** is an area in which selected characteristics are present throughout. It is also known as a uniform region or a homogeneous region. People in a politically-delineated area such as a county, state, or nation belong to a distinct formal region. Yet, although a substantial number of people of a certain characteristic live in such a region, there usually are others present (i.e. minorities) not described by the name and traits given to a formal region. This mixing of cultural identities is known as **diversity**. A **Functional Region** is a nodal area which influences and serves a larger area. The concentration of influence tends to be strongest at the core of the region and to decline with distance away from the core area. For example, the circulation of a newspaper is strongest in the city which it directly serves, and its circulation is less-strong outside of that particular town; it continues to descend until the influence of another town's newspaper is so strong that the previous newspaper isn't carried locally. A ***Vernacular Region (Perceptual Region)*** is one that is culturally identified by the people of some area. Examples of vernacular regions include the "Bible-belt," "Sun-belt," and "Frost-belt." Analysts are hard-pressed to uniformly outline a particular vernacular region; there are a multitude of perceptions for each region, owing to the numerous perceptions of any one labeled area by different groups of people.

Regional Integration (26-27): In the real world, geographers understand that characteristics are integrated. For example, geographers divide the world into two economic regions: ***More developed countries (MDC's)*** and ***Less developed countries (LDC's).*** MDC's such as those in Europe, U.S., Canada, and Japan reside mainly in the northern latitudes. Regions dominated by LDC's occupy mainly the southern latitudes. Consequently, there is a north-south partition of the world's social or economic problems. Geographers demonstrate the distribution of one trait of development in association with others. A primary objective of geographers is to understand better the areal associations of different regions.

Integrating Cancer Information (27-29): Geographers recognize that local environments may cause their residents to be affected by local physical phenomena. For example, core areas of water and air pollution seem to cause more people nearer the source to suffer greater from associated symptoms than do people located further away from the origin of the pollution. Maryland has the highest cancer rates among the fifty states. When cancer rates within Maryland are mapped, decisive internal variations may be observed. Westernmost Garret County has a 40 percent lower cancer rate than does Baltimore City (Fig. 1-11). Most of the high rates of cancer are in metro areas which, it turns out, are more inclined to suffer from air pollution and water pollution.

Spatial Analysis & Distribution (29): This concept emphasizes interactions among places. Also known as locational analysis, it searches for worldwide patterns in the distributions of human actions and environmental processes. The arrangement of any phenomenon across the Earth's surface is called ***spatial distribution***. Human activities and environmental conditions are dynamic, therefore the ***movement*** of people, goods, ideas, energy, and natural materials (like water) is a subject studied by geographers. Spatial distribution possesses three main components: density, concentration, and pattern.

Density, Concentration, and Pattern (29-31): The frequency with which something occurs in a measured area is called its ***density***. We can measure the density of doctors, teachers, police, diseases, cars, trees, and nearly anything else. ***Arithmetic density*** is the number of objects in a given area. For example, the arithmetic density of population in the UK is 240 persons per square mile. Some poorer countries such as China actually have lower arithmetic densities, not due to their small populations (China has well over a billion residents) but because of the even larger area in which their population lives. ***Physiological density*** measures the density of people in a country in relation to the arable land (land suited for agriculture). ***Agricultural density*** measures the number of farmers per unit area of cultivated farmland. The ***dispersion*** of something over an area is called ***concentration***. Things in a landscape are said to be *clustered* if they are found grouped in a small focal area. However, if objects are located far apart from each other they are *dispersed*. For example, the population of the United States has long been clustered in the North-East but, due to economic changes and aesthetic appreciation for warmer weather, the U.S.'s population density has increased in the Sun-belt and California. The final property of distribution is *pattern*, which is the geometric order by which the objects are set. Some objects are placed in a *regular, geometric* pattern while others are more *randomly* distributed. Some things such as cities can be seen in *linear* distributions as they are located along rivers, and others can be in a grid pattern such as the county lines and roads of the Mid-western plains.

Diffusion (31-34): The scattering of a phenomena across the landscape is referred to as *diffusion.* The original location from which an idea, technology, or whatever first disseminates upon a larger landscape is named a *hearth.* As an innovative idea emerges in one place, if well-enough received it will move onto other lands. Geography notes two basic types of diffusion: *Relocation* and *Expansion*. *Relocation diffusion* is the spread of a phenomena through the movement of people from one region to another area. The spread of a trait through a region (the people staying in place) is known as *expansion diffusion*. There are three types of expansion diffusion: *1-Hierarchical Diffusion, 2-Contagious Diffusion,* and *3-Stimulus Diffusion*. Hierarchical diffusion is the spread of phenomena from a node of origin. Contagious diffusion is the extensive diffusion of something through a population. It is analogous to the spread of a disease. Stimulus diffusion is the spread of an underlying principle, but not the specific idea. Due to quick transportation, computers, telecommunications, and e-mail systems, expansion diffusion can be achieved almost instantaneously. The reduction in the time it takes for an idea to disperse is called *space-time compression.*

Interaction (34-36): *Spatial interaction* describes the movement of people, goods, and ideas within and among regions. When there are large distances separating two groups, communication and interaction eventually deteriorate to complete isolation through the centuries. This decline in contact as time progresses is referred to as *distance decay*. When two groups attain a higher degree of interaction, the stronger and more influential culture will greatly affect the development of the other culture–a concept known as *acculturation*. When acculturation occurs, the weaker culture can either be completely replaced with the dominant culture, or it may be become greatly modified, with old features of the former society surviving within the framework of the newer, more influential culture. Some primitive tribes in remote areas of the world were so impressed with the arrival of humans in airplanes or ships that they were worshipped as gods. Such adoration for technology from advanced societies is termed *Cargo Cult*.

Globalization of Culture (36-38): Actions or processes that provide worldwide accessibility of something are called *globalization*. With freer trade, people around the world have more access to a greater diversity of goods; innovations in communications allow people to share ideas, knowledge, and concepts more readily. Such things integrate the world's environments, economies, and peoples, thus *"shrinking"* the world. *Culture* is the body of customary beliefs, social forms, and material traits constituting a distinct complex of tradition of a racial, religious, or social group. *Customary beliefs* affect population growth, religion, and food. *Social forms* are represented by language and non-verbal communication. *Material traits* depict a society's food, clothing, and shelter. *Uniform consumption preferences* may result when the television sets feed billions of people around the world similar information on products; the tastes of the world are often somewhat fused. For example, today there are many culturally different people on the planet who yearn for Nikes, jeans, and Sony electronic products. *Enhanced communications* result where travel is much quicker than in earlier times (Fig. 1-16). Also, telecommunications and computers make inter-global communication instantaneous and seemingly limitless. Still, many people in the world don't have access to the media and computer networks to the same degree as people in MDC's. Consequently, intellectual and economic disparities derived from this resource have increased the socio-economic disparities between LDC's and MDC's.

Globalization of Economy (38-40): In today's world, many large businesses place parts of their companies all around the world, depending upon where each will be most profitable. For one firm, manufacturing could be in Mexico, marketing could be in the U.S., and headquarters could remain in Amsterdam. These traits are linked to better transportation and communication, as well as to the globalization of the world's economy. At least one of the three financial centers of the world–*New York, Tokyo,* or *London*–is open nearly 24 hours a day, with differing schedules and time-zone differences. Firms that manufacture their goods, conduct research, and sell products in many different domains around the world are known as *transnational corporations*. Most transnational corporations are based in North America (mainly U.S.), Western Europe, and Japan. Current trends show that transnational corporations move many operations to countries where labor is comparatively less-expensive. For example, Fila (a shoe company) is traditionally Italian, but 90 percent of its sportswear is produced in Asian countries. With more competition brought forth from freer trade in the world, firms have spread their operations to places which are most profitable. Some factories are closed, and reopened in places with cheaper expenses (due to lower labor cost or less government interference).

Global Environment (40-44): *Resources* are things that yield value or are useful. People, fossil fuels, solar energy, trees, and water are a few examples of resources. The proper utilization of our resources is a constant source of debate among the globe's people. Long-term weather conditions at a particular place are known as its *climate*. The German climatologist *Vladamir Koppen* said the world was host to five different climate types: *A-Tropical Climates, B-Dry Climates, C- Warm Mid-Latitude Climates, D-Cold Mid-Latitude Climates,* and *E- Polar Climates*. Humans aren't adept at living in places with extremes of rainfall or temperature. The map in Fig. 2-1 shows that people are less attracted by weather that is too wet, too cold, too hot, or too dry. In Southwestern India, Bangladesh, and Myanmar (formerly Burma), *monsoon* rains come each year to replenish the water supplies, and usually flood many parts of the area. The Monsoons of South Asia last from *June through September* and provide the area with water and (due to flooding) widespread fertilizer (silt) for their crops. Most of the Earth's land surfaces support some type of vegetation communities, called *biomes*. Earth's vegetation consist of four biomes. **1)** In the *forest biome* trees form a continuous canopy over the ground. Forest biomes are found in

8

North America, Europe, Asia, and the tropical areas of South America, Africa, and Southeast Asia. **2)** The *savanna biome* is a mixture of trees and grasses that are prominent in Africa, South Asia, South America, and Australia. **3)** *Grassland biomes* cover much of North America and don't support many trees due to lack of precipitation. **4)** *Desert biomes* do support some plants and animals which have adapted to dry environments. The natural terrestrial surface layer containing living matter and supporting–or capable of supporting– plants is known as *soil*. *Erosion* and the *depletion of nutrients* are the main agents that tend to destroy soil. The science that studies Earth's landforms is called *geomorphology*. *Relief* is the difference in elevation between two points. *Slope* is the angle at which land is inclined. Slope and relief are shown on topographic maps, which are used to study physical and cultural features of landscapes (Fig. 1-8).

Human Modification of the Environment (44-47): Good and bad examples are found in the Netherlands and Florida. Few places on the planet have been modified to benefit people as much as the polders of the Netherlands. A *polder* is a piece of land that has been created by draining water from an area, and then encircling it with dikes to prevent it from becoming periodically flooded. A *dike* is an elongated dam that prevents water from lakes or the ocean from flooding areas of lower elevation. Like much of the Netherlands, New Orleans is protected by dikes, because much of its topography lies below the water level of the Mississippi River. The Dutch have been transforming the North Sea into land in this way since around 1200 A.D., mainly in the *Zuider Zee Works* and the *Delta Plan*, the two primary polder projects in the Netherlands. The famous windmills associated with the Netherlands used to be widely used for pumping water from polder areas. Once dried, the polder can be used for construction, agriculture, or recreation. Due to periodic flooding, the State of Florida asked the federal government to straighten the 98 mile-long *Kissimmee River* which meandered from Orlando to Lake Okeechobee (Fig. 1-21). During times when annual flooding was great, the river would immerse 45,000 acres of nearby land, much under agricultural production. In 1971, the channel opened and changed the environmental landscape of Florida. Water drained from cattle farms defiled the canal. The river, in turn, polluted and fouled Lake Okeechobee, the source of fresh water for half of the state's population. Since then the Army Corps of Engineers has spent hundreds of millions of dollars in attempts to rectify their mistake, by restoring the river to its original course. Barrier islands run parallel to the coast of the southern and eastern states of the U.S.. People build homes upon them for the view and aesthetics of a nearby ocean. However, with human occupancy erosion is exacerbated, and many of the homes are periodically destroyed by storms.

CLOSING REMARKS

The concepts presented in Chapter One impart an understanding of how geography was developed historically, how geographers answer the "Where" and "Why" questions, and how the human-environment and regional studies methods answer the "Why" questions of geography. It is very important to learn the ideas presented in this introductory chapter; future chapters in Rubenstein build upon its foundation in the fundamentals of geography. If any one component of this chapter incites a special curiosity, be assured that more detailed description of related material is likely be found in one of the remaining twelve chapters of the book.

KEY TERMS AND CONCEPTS

Geography: The scientific study of the location of people and activities across the Earth's surface, and the reasons for their distribution.

Map: A two-dimensional, or flat representation of the Earth's surface, or a portion of it. It can be used to show physical traits of the landscape, or to display thematic data.

Cartography: The science of making maps. In the past most were made largely by hand but, with computers and software, they are now mostly created electronically.

Scale: The relationship between the size of an object on a map, and that object's true dimensions on the Earth. Large-scale maps show great detail over small areas; small-scale maps show less detail over large areas.

Projection: The system used to transfer locations from the globe onto a map. Projections invariably distort the size or shape of areas.

Mercator Projection: It shows all meridians and parallels intersecting at right angles. Additionally, lands in polar regions are unrealistically immense.

Equator: The parallel with the greatest diameter; it splits the Earth into two hemispheres (half spheres)–the Northern and Southern Hemispheres.

Latitude: The numbering system used to indicate the location of parallels drawn on a globe and measured in degrees north and south of the equator, the equator being zero degrees.

Parallels: Circles drawn around the globe parallel to the equator which intersect meridians at right angles. All points upon them lie equally distant from the equator (and from the poles).

Longitude: The numbering system used to indicate the location meridians drawn on a globe and measuring distance east and west of the Prime Meridian, which is the base meridian for the system used in most places.

Prime Meridian: The meridian which passes through the Royal Observatory in Greenwich, England; it is designated as 0 degrees.

Remote Sensing: The process by which images (captured by electronic equipment in satellites and airplanes) can be used to observe and analyze the Earth's surface.

Geographic Information System: Computer software that facilitates the storage, analysis, and display of geographic data, usually as an integrated series of map coverages (layers).

Vasco Nunez de Balboa: The first European to view the Pacific; the year was 1513.

Ferdinand Magellan: His ship, the "Victoria," was the first to sail around the world. He was killed in the Philippines by hostile natives. The Straits of Magellan near Cape Horn, South America are named in his honor.

Environmental Determinism: An approach to the study of geography (very popular in the nineteenth and early twentieth-century) which argued that general laws sought by human geographers could be found using approaches developed in the physical sciences. Geography was, therefore, the study of how the physical environment determined human activities.

Possibilism: The twentieth-century theory that the physical environment may set limits on human actions, but people have the ability to adjust to the physical environment and choose their courses of action from many alternatives.

Location: The position on the Earth's surface that an object occupies. The location of something answers the "Where" question.

Toponym: Literally this term means "place name," and it is used to describe a place on the Earth's surface.

Site: The physical character of a location. Climate, soil, elevations, and others characteristics associated with a place describe its site.

Situation: The location of a place relative to other places. By using the locations of known places as reference points, the locations of unfamiliar localities may be more effectively presented.

Mathematical Location: A system that uses lines of longitude and latitude to specify the location of a place lying on the Earth's surface.

U.S. Land Ordinance of 1785: A system based upon Principal Meridians and Baselines which divided unsettled areas of the U.S. into uniformly 36 square mile townships. In turn each square mile or section was quartered into 160 acre plots, which were the base size for most homesteading.

Region: An area distinguished by one or more distinctive characteristics. Areas with similar climates, agriculture practices, or religions may be classified as a region.

The Regional Analysis Tradition of Geography: This is a way of organizing the study of the Earth's peoples and environments through identification of regions and their descriptions, based upon similarities and differences and the magnitudes thereof.

Formal Region: An area in which a selected characteristic is present throughout (a.k.a. uniform or homogeneous region). Cities, states, and nations are formal regions, due to many uniform traits they possess.

Diversity: Even in a "homogeneous" region there are minorities within that region or culture that deviate from the stated rule. These additional cultures add more flavors to the final cultural product of a society. These influences represent the diversity of a region.

Functional Region: An area in which an activity has a focal point. The characteristic dominates at a central node; it diffuses toward the outer part of the region, diminishing and eventually disappearing.

Vernacular Region (Perceptual Region): An area that people believe to exist as part of their cultural identity. For example, "Dixie" is the name that many people give to most parts of the former Civil War Confederacy, though it has no government or specific delineation.

More Developed Countries: Countries that are more developed economically. These countries tend to be found in Western Europe, North America (U.S. & Canada), and East Asia (Japan).

Less Developed Countries: Countries that are less developed economically. They are also called "developing countries." High birth rates, low income, lower literacy rates, and poorer health care tend to be traits of LDC's.

Spatial Distribution: The arrangement of a phenomenon across the Earth's surface. For example, population distribution across the Earth is clustered in many places and nearly non-existent in other, less-hospitable places.

Spatial Interaction: The movement of people, goods, and ideas within and among regions. With recent innovations in television, computers, and telephones spatial interaction has increased dramatically, thus rendering the planet "smaller."

Density: The frequency with which something occurs within a given unit of area. For example, the density of fast food restaurants would be greater in a college neighborhoods than in most non-college neighborhoods.

Arithmetic Density: This is the number of objects in a given area. For example, the arithmetic density of the UK is 240 persons per square mile.

Physiological Density: Measuring the density of people against arable land is physiological density. Japan has a large physiological density, due to its large population and small amount of arable land.

Agricultural Density: The number of farmers per unit area of cultivated farmland is agricultural density.

Concentration: The extent of spread of a phenomenon over a given area. For example, much of the U.S. population is concentrated in the Northeast, around the Great Lakes, and in southern California.

Pattern: The geometric arrangement of something. Regular, random, and linear are the three main types of patterns.

Diffusion: The process of spread across the landscape.

Hearth: The region from which original ideas originate. For example: Paris, New York, Milan, and Tokyo are fashion clothing hearths, because many new types of clothing are first introduced in these cities.

Relocation Diffusion: The spread of an idea through migration of people from one region to another. For example, when French traders and settlers brought their language to Eastern Canada they were practicing relocation diffusion of the French language.

Expansion Diffusion: The spread of a characteristic among people within a region. It is divided into three components: 1-Hierarchical Diffusion: the spread of an idea that originates at a node of innovation within a region to other nodes in the hierarchy. 2-Contagious Diffusion: the widespread diffusion of a characteristic throughout a population (as in a disease). 3-Stimulus Diffusion: the spread of an underlying principle, even though a characteristic, itself, fails to diffuse.

Space-time Compression: The reduction in time required for an idea to disperse. Increases in technology and its utilization increase this phenomena.

Distance Decay: The characteristic decrease of influence of a phenomenon with distance away from the place(s) where that phenomenon is found.

Acculturation: The modification of a culture as result of contact with another (usually a more powerful) culture. Even so, often the less dominant culture will inject some of its traits into the more dominant culture, as in the infusion of African-influenced music into the mainstream of the U.S..

Cargo Cult: A belief that the arrival of a ship or airplane in a locality has spiritual meaning.

Globalization: Actions or processes that provide worldwide accessibility to something. Technology and its utilization increase levels of globalization.

Culture: The body of customary beliefs, social forms, and material traits constituting a distinct complex of tradition of a racial, religious, or social group.

Uniform Consumption Preferences: Products that are desired due to their utility and fashion, often represented by a complex structure of marketing mechanisms.

Financial Centers of the World: New York, Tokyo, and London have tremendous influences upon the financial structure of the global economy.

Transnational Corporations: Firms which locate different parts of their organization in various places in the world, due to the comparative advantages of those places.

Resources: Things that yield value or are useful. People, fossil fuels, solar energy, trees, and water are all examples of resources.

Climate: The long-term weather of a particular region. Climates are greatly influenced by latitude, elevation, and relative location in relation to mountains, bodies of waters, and ocean currents.

Monsoon: The wind patterns that affect South Asia blowing landward in the summer (bringing rains) and seaward in the winter (rendering drought).

Biomes: A large community of Earth's land vegetation. Included are the 1-forest biome, 2-savanna biome, 3-grassland biome, and 4-desert biome.

Soil: The material that lies on Earth's surface between the air and rocks. It contains living matter and is capable of supporting plants.

Erosion: The removal of mineral particles and/or soil from bedrock by rain, ice, wind, or water.

Geomorphology: The study of Earth's landforms.

Relief: The difference in elevation between two points. Relief measures the extent to which an area is flat or hilly.

Slope: Relief divided by the distance between two points: slope measure the steepness of hills.

Polder: Land created by the Dutch by draining water from an areas formerly covered by shallow seas or lakes.

Dikes: An elongated dam that encircles polders and prevents flooding by restraining rivers, oceans, seas, and lakes. Currently also applied to any elongated dam along a river course.

1. The scientific study of the locations of people and activities
across the Earth's _____ is known as _____.   Surface, Geography

2. Geography is divided into two realms: _____ Geography and   Physical,
_____ Geography   Human

3. A _____ is a graphic representation of an area on Earth's   map
surface.

4. _____-scale maps have large denominators and display less   Small,
detail but large areas, while _____-scale maps have small   large
denominators and display more detail but small areas.

5. Halfway between the poles exists the _____ which divides the Equator,
world into two hemispheres, the _____ Hemisphere and the   Northern, Southern
_____ Hemisphere.

6. The Earth's _____ is about 40,000 kilometers (25,000 miles), circumference,
while its _____ is about 12, 875 kilometers (8,000 miles).   diameter

7. The science and art of creating maps is known as _____.   Cartography

8. _____ collect data from outer space. _____ _____ is the   Satellites, Remote
science of processing and displaying this geographical data.   Sensing

9. _____ _____ _____ are software packages that can integrate   Geographic Information
and manipulate different sets of geographic data in map formats. Systems

10. In _____ projections size is greatly distorted in the polar Mercator
latitudes.

11. The Greek, _____, was the first person acknowledged to use   Eratosthenes
the word "Geography."

12. Ptolemy wrote the eight-volume _____ to _____.   Guide, Geography

13. Juan Sebastian del Cano brought the _____ into port in Spain Victoria,
after a circumnavigation of Earth. The original captain, _____, Magellan,
was killed back in the islands today known as the _____.   Philippines

14. Alexander Von Humbolt and _____ _____ brought geography into the _____ era by introducing methods of _____ inquiry to geography.

Carl Ritter, modern, scientific

15. Environmental determinism is the concept that says the physical environment determines _____ _____.

social development

16. _____ is the idea that the environment may limit some human actions, but people can adjust to their surroundings.

Possibilism

17. Ellen Churchill Semple subscribed to the _____ _____ theory of human development.

environmental determinism

18. _____ is the name given to something's position on the surface of Earth.

Location

19. A _____ or perceptual region is one culturally identified by the people of some area.

vernacular

20. The arrangement of anything across the Earth's surface is its _____ _____.

spatial distribution

21. Physiological density measures the number of people within a country against the country's _____ _____.

arable land

22. A _____ is another word for place name.

toponym

23. The physical characteristics of a place are said to be its _____.

site

24. The farther you go away from the location of something, the less influence it is likely to have. This is called _____ _____.

distance decay

25. Earth's system of parallels originates at the _____.

Equator

26. Lines of Longitude always intersect parallels at _____ angles.

right

27. Zero degrees longitude is known as the _____ _____.

Prime Meridian

28. The International Date Line lies mostly along _____ _____.

180° longitude

29. A survey township consists of _____ square miles.

36

30. Homesteaders generally staked out _____ acres of land, which is __/__ of a section.

160, 1/4

31. Vegetation communities of the Earth are called _____.   biomes

32. _____ is the science that studies Earth's landforms.   Geomorphology

33. In South Asia, the _____ bring rains primarily during the _____ season.   monsoon, summer

34. A dike is elongated dam which keeps oceans, lakes, rivers, and seas from _____ areas of lower _____.   flooding, elevation

35. _____ _____ conduct different segments of business in many different nations throughout the world.   Transnational corporations

36. Actions or processes that provide the world with higher levels of accessibility is known as _____.   globalization

CHAPTER TWO

POPULATION

OVERVIEW

Population growth and decline, rationalizations for population growth, the spatial distribution of people on Earth, differing regional population growth rates, and the prospect of the planet facing an overpopulation dilemma are the main ideas presented in Chapter Two. When geographers, engineers, planners, and other professionals strategically plan cities, infrastructures, economies, and other important elements of society they must have a good idea of how many people will be using such resources in the future, else there will be waste. When the number of people in an area exceeds the carrying capacity of the land there is often hunger, poverty, and lower standards of living. In today's world there are many examples of such traits in countries that are classified as Less developed countries (LDC's). Countries which generally have lower rates of population increase are classified as More developed countries (MDC's). The population dynamics and distributions submitted in Chapter Two provide a basis for a better understanding of why economies flourish or flounder, why people in certain areas retain higher living standards than others, and why governments are hard pressed to aid their populaces.

SELECTED NOTES

Population Study and Its Importance (59): Population analysis is very important for three reasons: *1-six billion* people inhabit the Earth, far more than at any other time in the planet's history; *2*-during the past fifty years the population has *increased faster* than at any other time in history; and *3*-nearly all population growth is found within poor, developing countries. *Demography* is the scientific study of population characteristics. Demographers contemplate cartographically and statistically how people and traits of income, gender, occupation, and health are spread about the world, at differing levels of geography. In so doing, demographers answer questions in a wide array of areas that may not be known otherwise. Geographers argue, using the human-environment approach, that *overpopulation* is not a simple equation between the number of people in the world and its area, but has many other variables which, when used properly, give an idea of the ability of an area's people to be sustained by their available resources. Using the *regional analysis* approach, geographers find that some areas and nations of the Earth can readily support their populations while others cannot.

Population Concentrations in the World (59): The world has two general areas which either accommodate human occupancy or retard them. About *75%* of the Earth's population live on only *5%* of its land area. Two thirds of the world's population live within 500 kilometers of an ocean, while eighty percent of the population live within 800 kilometers of it. They tend not to live in the remote interiors of continents. People tend to live in low-lying areas with fertile soil, and temperate climates. Five population clusters contain most of Earth's human occupants: *1-East Asia, 2-South Asia, 3-Southeast Asia, 4-Western Europe,* and *5-Eastern North America.* (See Figure 2.1 for a world map of population distribution.).

Asia's Three Clusters of Population (59-62): Approximately one-fourth of the world's people (1.5 billion) live in *East Asia,* the *largest cluster* of inhabitants in the world. Five-sixths of the people in this concentration reside in the *People's Republic of China*, the world's most populous country. China only ranks third in the world in terms of area. Still, most of its people live near the Pacific coast and in several fertile river valleys that drain the interior of the country. Seventy-five percent of its people live in rural areas and work as farmers. In *Japan*, 25 percent of the people live in two urban areas that accounts for only three percent of its land area. *South Asia* has the second largest concentration of people. Over 20 percent of the world's inhabitants are found here. *India, Bangladesh, Pakistan,* and *Sri Lanka* form the bulk of land area and population in South Asia. Most South Asians are farmers living in rural areas, like in China. Only twenty-five percent of the people live in urban areas. *Southeast Asia* is the fourth-largest (after Africa) population cluster in the world. Indonesia, the world's fourth most populous country, is in this cluster, as are the Philippines. Like China and South Asia, most of its inhabitants are found working as farmers in rural areas.

Europe and Eastern North America (62-63): Europe and Russia contain nearly *fifteen* percent of the world's overall population. This region includes over two dozen countries varying greatly in size from Monaco to Russia. Unlike most of Asia, three-fourths of this region's people live in cities, while less than twenty percent are farmers. The highest concentrations of people are in the coal fields of England, Germany, and Belgium, historically the centers of energy for industry. Eastern North America includes the northeastern U.S. and southeastern Canada and possesses about 150 million people. Like Europeans, they tend to be urban dwellers and fewer than five percent are employed in agriculture.

Dry Lands & Wet Lands (63): Extremely dry and wet lands are not inviting to human occupation for they tend to retard agriculture. Regions too dry for farming cover approximately twenty percent of Earth's land surface. The two large desert regions of the Earth extend from 10 to 50 degrees north and south of the equator. The largest desert in the world extends from North Africa to Central Asia and is known as the Sahara, Arabian, Gobi, and Takla Makan deserts. Deserts generally lack sufficient water to support crops that could sustain large populations. Some people, however, do survive by raising animals such as camels. Wet lands receiving extreme amounts of precipitation are dually inhospitable to human occupation. They are located in the tropics between twenty degrees north and south latitude, covering equatorial regions. Rainfall in these areas average more than fifty inches per year with most receiving more than 90 inches. Nutrients are rapidly depleted from the soil due to moisture and heat, hindering agriculture. Still, in Southeast Asia rice is grown in the wet season and sustains a large population.

Cold & High Lands (63): Much of the land near the poles of the Earth is perpetually frozen (permafrost), covered with ice and snow, or both. Consequently, the land cannot support crops; only a few, hardy animals and people live there. Relatively few people live in the mountainous regions of the world. However, one exception is the preeminent metropolitan area known as Mexico City, which is situated at an elevation of 7,300 feet.

Three Types of Density (65-68): Density is the number of people occupying a specified amount of land. Here three different measures of density are presented. *Arithmetic density* is the total number of people divided by the entire land area. It is the most basic form of density assessment in this trio. *Physiological density* measures the total population of an area in relation to that area's arable land. Arable land is ground suitable for agricultural production. This assessment gives a good, general idea in regards to the ability of a region to sustain its inhabitants with food. The final density computation is *Agricultural density* (the number of farmers per unit of arable land). MDC's such as the U.S. and Canada have very low agricultural densities due to the very efficient farming methods practiced. However, LDC's such as India and China have higher agricultural densities.

Three Revolutions That Increased World Population(68-70): Until about 8000 B.C. the global population had only increased slightly in any given year. Innovations which dramatically increased the number of people living on the planet had yet to be introduced. Three major "Revolutions" developed concepts that ultimately led to a larger number of people living on the planet. The first was the *agricultural revolution* that began around 8000 B.C. which led humans to domesticate plants and animals, thus relieving them of their total dependence on hunting and gathering techniques. In so doing, the human population found a food source that was dually more bountiful and more predictable than previous methods. Such nutritional advances encouraged survival and reproduction. The *industrial revolution* occurred around 1750 A.D.. After this time the world's population grew ten times faster than it had in the past. During this time there were innovations such as the steam engine, mass production, and powered transportation. The result of these inventions were unprecedented levels of wealth in many countries, which led to better food supplies and healthier infrastructures in the way of sanitation and public utilities. Around 1950, the *medical revolution* began dispersing medical technology invented in Europe and North America to the poorer countries of Latin America, Asia, and Africa. Consequently, the populations of these continents suddenly had much lower Crude death rates than the past, which, coupled with still high Crude birth rates, lead to a population explosion, which is still expanding. No longer did such diseases as smallpox, influenza, malaria, and tuberculosis claim large segments of the population every year.

Rates of Natural Increase (70-72): In order to best measure population growth, demographers and geographers identify factors that directly cause the human populace to shrink or swell. In simplest terms, Earth's population is most affected by fertility and mortality. The **Rate of natural increase (RNI)** is the percentage by which the population grows in a given year. It is calculated by subtracting the Crude death rate from the Crude birth rate in a given year. The **RNI** for the world during the past decade was 1.7 percent. In order to find out how quickly a given population will double simply divide 70 (a constant term) by the RNI. For example, if the RNI is 2 percent then the population will double in approximately 35 years. *Doubling Time = 70 / RNI*. Small changes in RNI such as a tenth of a percent in increase can have long term effects on population size. RNI's vary greatly from region to region (Fig. 2-4). In LDC's such as Africa and Southwestern Asia RNI's are high at 3.0 percent. Yet in MDC's such as the U.S., Canada, Europe, and Japan their respective RNI's are much lower, below one percent. Several European countries would experience negative population rates if it weren't for immigrants that supplement their populations. Virtually all of the Earth's population growth takes place in LDC's.

Fertility and Mortality (72-75): The *crude birth rate (CBR)* is the number of births per year for every 1,000 people in society. Likewise, the number of deaths per thousand people per year is referred to as the *crude death rate (CDR)*. The *total fertility rate (TFR)* is the measurement of the total number of births. The average number of children a woman will have between the ages of 14 and 49 (her child bearing years) is the TFR. Large CBR's tend to correlate with high RNI's (Fig. 2-4, 2-5). The *infant mortality rate* is the annual number of deaths of infants less than one year old. It is usually expressed as the number of deaths per 1,000 births in the first year of life. High infant mortality rates are found in LDC's and, logically, lower rates of death among infants exist in MDC's which provide better health care and nutrition to their infants due to higher income levels. When babies are born they can expect to live a certain number of years according to the mortality levels existing in their region of the world. This is known as *life expectancy*. Europeans and Americans can expect to live into their late seventies while most Africans will only live into their early fifties. Due to variance among population in regards to age, CDR's may be somewhat deceptive in terms of how well a society cares for its populace.

The Demographic Transition, Stages 1 & 2 (75-76): As time progresses so do the dynamics associated with population growth. The three revolutions spoken of earlier had profound effects upon the growth rates of the nations of the world. The process of change from high birth and death rates to low birth and death rates is known as the *demographic transition*. There are four stages in this transition and they are shown in Figure 2-9. *Stage 1* of the demographic transition is characterized by high CBR's as well as high CDR's with an RNI near "0." Most of human history and prehistory were spent in this period because food sources were not plentiful due to hunting and gathering or primitive farming methods. In *Stage 2*, there is high population growth; the CBR remains high while the CDR plummets because technology has increased food supplies and reduced disease. Europe and the U.S. experienced this stage in the late 1700's and early 1800's. Many LDC's have been experiencing Stage 2 only since the late 1900's.

The Demographic Transition, Stages 3 & 4 (76-78): When the CDR drops sharply, a country begins to experience *Stage 3* of the demographic transition. The CDR continues to fall in Stage 3, but much slower than in Stage 2. In this stage the difference between CBR and CDR narrows somewhat, thus slowing the RNI. Europe and North America entered this stage in the early twentieth century while some LDC's in Africa, Asia, and Latin America have progressed to Stage 3 in recent years. In Stage 3, children are not economic assets, thus they are not produced in such large numbers as in the previous stages of the demographic transition. When the CBR approaches the CDR a country's RNI once again approaches zero. At this point, a country has entered *Stage 4* of the demographic transition. A very low RNI is known as *zero population growth*. In terms of total fertility rate, 2.1 is the number of births needed to replace the population and not add growth. However, if a country has a significant number of immigrants annually, a TFR of 2.1 may still lead to some growth. *Several European countries have reached Stage 4* of the demographic transition including Sweden, Germany, and the United Kingdom. The U.S. remains in Stage 3 because birth rates are still somewhat high among some groups. Factors leading to lower birth rates include more available sources of birth control, more career-minded women, a yearning for the kinds of leisure time inconsistent with having children, and economic considerations which view children as a barrier to financial stability. A country starts in Stage 1 with low growth and, eventually, ends up in Stage 4 with low growth. But, meanwhile, their population grows rapidly in stages two and three of the transition.

England's Demographic Transition (78-79): England is a good case study for demographic transition because its boundaries have remained static for centuries and it hasn't been greatly affected by immigration. Plagues and poor harvests kept England in Stage 1 until about 1750 A.D. (See Fig. 2-10). Between 1750 and 1880 England profited from the Industrial revolution and spent much money on improvements in health and better food supplies, and its population grew rapidly. England had an average growth rate of 1.4 percent during this period. England was in Stage 3 from 1880 to the early 1970's; there was moderate growth of 0.7 percent per year. Since the early 1970's England's growth has only been 0.1 percent annually, which means England has been in Stage 4 since that time. Again, England experiences little growth, having now achieved low birth and death rates generally associated with MDC's.

Population Pyramids (79-82): Different stages of the demographic transition mean that the population's structure will vary accordingly. The distribution of age and gender groups in a population are effectively displayed in a *Population pyramid (Fig. 2-11)*. The pyramid usually depicts the population in five-year increments, beginning with ages 0 to 4 at the base and moving ever higher to the oldest age group at the top of the pyramid. The ratio of males to females in a society is known as the *sex ratio*. Males occupy the left side of the scale and females the right. More males are born than females but males don't survive as long, on average. Thus, men outnumber women until about age thirty, at which time women begin numerical superiority. So it is that in the U.S. overall, there are 95 men for every 100 women, which means the median age of a person in the U.S. must be greater

than 30. People who are 0-14 and over 65 are considered outside of the work force.
Those 15 to 64 are determined to be productive workers. So, the ratio between these two
groups is the **dependency ratio**. In Stage 2 of the transition the dependency ratio is 1:1
(one dependent for one worker) and in Stage 4 it is 1:2 (one dependent for every two
workers). Thus the burden for workers is only half as great in Stage 2 than in Stage 4 of
the Population pyramid.

Countries In Different Stages of Demographic Transition (82-85): ***Cape Verde*** remained
in Stage 1 of the demographic transition until the late 1940's. Between 1900 and 1949 its
population actually declined from 147,000 to 137,000. Births did exceed deaths in most
years, but severe famines caused the long-term population decline. However, anti-malarial
campaigns and more secure food supplies tripled the country's population to 400,000 since
1950. With an annual RNI of 3 percent, Cape Verde remains in Stage 2. Since about
1960 ***Chile*** has been in Stage 3 of the Population pyramid. Its CDR dropped sharply to
about 10 by the 1970's and its CBR declined to about 20 by the late 1970's. But, Chileans
like to have large families, consistent with the Catholic Church's doctrine and Spanish
culture. So, it appears as though it will be a long time before Chile enters Stage 4.
Denmark has reached Stage 4. Its population pyramid is more like a column than a
pyramid, indicating that the percentage of elderly citizens is more or less equal to its
younger population. Since the 1970's the CBR's and CDR's have been equal at about 12
per 1,000.

Demographic Transition and World Population Growth (85-86): The world's
demographic transition is like the different nations so far described, but on a much larger
scale. The first break in the Population pyramid, the huge drop in the death rate, has
occurred nearly everywhere. In Europe and the U.S. this transformation took place long
ago, whereas in most countries in the world it has occurred during the twentieth century,
and much more quickly. The second break, a drop in the birth rate, has yet to be achieved
in many countries. Therefore, population is still increasing rapidly in those countries. If
the nations of Asia, Africa, and Latin America take 100 years to pass through Stage 2 as
did Europe and the U.S., their populations won't stabilize until the year 2050 A.D., at
which time 15 billion people will be living on Earth!

Malthus on Overpopulation (86-87): ***Thomas Malthus (1766-1834)*** was an English
economist who was concerned with the growth of human population. His essay published
in 1798, ***"An Essay on the Principle of Population**,"* was concerned with the theorized
inability of the human population to feed itself due to overpopulation. According to
Malthus, *food supplies grew only arithmetically while population expanded*
geometrically (increasingly faster than arithmetically). He warned that starvation would
reduce the human race's numbers unless moral restraint, natural disasters, or disease
slowed the RNI first.

Malthus's Critics & Neo-Malthusians (87-88): Many critics disagree with Malthus's essay.
Friedrich Engels, a noted founding Communist, dismissed Malthus's theory as a
capitalistic endeavor that didn't consider the egalitarian distribution of resources as an

alternative to starvation. *Julian Simon*, an economist, disagreed with Malthus because he believed that an expanding population would build a better economy and develop more ideas to improve agriculture and design innovations. Geographer *Vaclav Smith* determined that, since 1950, food production growth has actually out-distanced human reproduction. Still, given the time in which Malthus lived, he did have grand foresight since only a couple of countries had entered Stage 2 during that era. With rapidly expanding RNI's that exist today, many people have adopted Malthus's cause yet again. These *Neo-Malthusians* include *Robert Kaplan and Thomas Faser Homer-Dixon*. They believe that as resources become scarce, due to competition, humans will vigorously compete for what is left of clean air, fuel, wood, and other resources. One target example of Neo-Malthusian thought is East Africa where population growth outpaced that of income three percent to two percent. Countries in East Africa are worse off now than they were a decade ago, in part because economic growth has not been as great as population growth.

Reducing Natural Increase (88-90): To decrease population growth, either the CDR must rise or the CBR must be lowered. Many people believe that sending food to the starving just sustains a highly reproductive population. Eventually, a catastrophic starvation will occur, just as Malthus predicted, slowing population. Disease rates are still relatively high in LDC's and, due to mutations in viruses and bacteria, these diseases could overcome the inoculations that have so far been developed. AIDS is also on the rise in LDC's and MDC's. AIDS is growing in number of people affected and in its areal domain; it is not medically controlled and it continues to spread. The second school of thought on reducing the population advocates lowering the birth rate. This can be done by increasing women's standards of living in the world, increasing access to birth control, and education. Still, there is opposition to many forms of birth control, especially by adherents of various religions found throughout the world. The most controversial is abortion, opposed by many people, especially in the U.S..

Case Studies, India & China (91-94): *China and India* are the two most populous countries in the world. However, due to India's less effective family planning it adds two million more people each year than does China. By the middle of the next century it will probably overtake China as the world's most populous country. After India broke from the UK in 1947, its death rate dropped sharply, thus increasing the country's population dramatically. Currently, family planning in India has been weak, mainly because the citizens are worried about forced sterilization and retain an aversion to birth control. Unlike India, China has been quite effective in its development of family planning. The government's role has been to limit the number of children per family to one. This policy did encourage *infanticide* (killing of babies); since most families hold male babies in higher regard in China, female infanticide was especially high. As China moves into a market economy, it realizes that having fewer children is economically viable, freeing up capital to raise living standards.

CLOSING REMARKS

Overpopulation has already affected many parts of Africa, Latin America, and Asia. In these places, high population growth stresses the environment and forces economies into worsening conditions. The sheer number of people living in a certain area is not necessarily an indication of overpopulation. However, the ability of those people to work successfully with their environment and economy may be just such an indication. An expanding population can improve some economic conditions; out-of-control growth causes tremendous stress to the resources of many countries, depressing the living standards of many if not most of their citizens. Due to the agricultural, industrial, and medical revolutions in innovation, population has increased dramatically in the world. While some regions experienced rapid growth rates two-hundred years ago, many are encountering dramatic increases presently. Research tends to suggest the RNI's of the faster-growing countries should be lowered, but differ philosophically about how a lower RNI should be achieved.

KEY TERMS AND CONCEPTS

Demography: The scientific study of population characteristics. In contemporary society computer software allows many intricate studies of this nature to be performed using mapping and statistical packages.

Census: A complete enumeration of a population. In the U.S., our national population census is taken every ten years, at the beginning of new decades.

Overpopulation: The number of people in an area exceeds the capacity of the environment to support life at a decent standard of living. Many ecologists and environmentalists believe this phenomena has drastic effects on Earth's biosphere.

Arithmetic Density: The total number of people divided by the total land area; the basic form of density at which national comparisons are most often made.

Physiological Density: The number of people per unit of area of arable land, which is land suitable for agriculture. Physiological density indicates the ability of a country's agriculture to sustain the population in food products.

Agricultural Density: The ratio of the number of farmers to the total amount of land suitable for agriculture. In MDC's this figure is normally quite low, but in LDC's the agricultural density is distinctively higher.

Agricultural Revolution: When human beings first domesticated plants and animals and no longer relied entirely on hunting and gathering. The agricultural revolution first appeared about 8,000 B.C. and resulted in more complex societies.

Industrial Revolution: A series of improvements in industrial technology that transformed the process of manufacturing goods. Europe, especially Great Britain, and the U.S. were the first regions in the world to benefit extensively from the riches of the industrial revolution.

Medical Revolution: Diffusion of medical technology invented in Europe and North America to the poorer countries of Latin America, Asia, and Africa. Due to the medical revolution, the Crude death rate dropped swiftly, increasing population growth rates in many parts of the world.

Natural Increase (Rate of Natural Increase, (RNI)): The percentage growth of population in a year, computed as the crude birth rate (CBR) subtracted from the Crude death rate (CDR). This value represents how quickly a given population is growing. For example, the world's population has grown at the rate of 1.7% annually during the last decade.

Doubling Time: The number of years needed to double a population, assuming a constant rate of natural increase. The formula is this: Doubling Time = 70 / RNI (%).

Crude Birth Rate (CBR): The total number of live births in a year for every 1,000 people alive in society. CBR's tend to be high in LDC's and low in MDC's.

Crude Death Rate (CDR): The total number of deaths in a year for every 1,000 people alive in the society. Deaths were greatly reduced by the Medical Revolution.

Total Fertility Rate: The average number of children a woman will have throughout her childbearing years. Women in LDC's tend to have more children than women in MDC's.

Infant Mortality Rate: The total number of deaths in a year among infants under one year old for every 1,000 live births in a society. In the U.S., the higher rates in inner cities rival some LDC's Infant Mortality Rates.

Life Expectancy: The average number of years an individual can be expected to live, given current social, economic, and medical conditions. Life expectancy at birth is a rough estimate of the average number of years a newborn infant can expect to live.

Demographic Transition: The process of change in a society's population from a condition of high crude birth and death rates and low rate of natural increase, to a condition of low crude birth and death rates, low rate of natural increase, and a higher total population. Sweden, Germany, and Denmark have reached the final stage of this demographic transition.

Zero Population Growth (ZPG): The total fertility rate declines to the point where the natural increase rate equals zero. At this rate human reproduction would serve to replace existing populations, without enlarging them.

Population Pyramid: A bar graph representing the distribution of population by age and sex. Countries with large young populations are pyramid in shape, whereas MDC's become more columnar as they reach Stage 4 of the demographic transition.

Sex Ratio: The number of men to women in a society. MDC's have larger female populations because women survive longer than do men.

Dependency Ratio: The number of people either under age 15 or over age 64, compared to the number of people active in the labor force. High dependency ratios cause stress to the strength of a country's economy.

Thomas Malthus: An English economist who wrote the essay "An Essay on the Principle of Population" which theorized that food production on a world scale would be unable to serve the exploding populations of Earth, thus leading to mass starvation.

According to Malthus, food supplies grew only arithmetically while population grew geometrically.

Infanticide: The deliberate killing of infants. In some cultures male babies are more highly prized than females. Due to the financial inability of many families to sustain numerous children, the killing of less desirable children (who are most often female) sometimes occurs.

Population Control Policies: Government's legal position on birth control. India's efforts to stem population growth have been less successful than those of China. China penalizes families who have more than one child.

CHAPTER TWO

1. The population of Earth is currently over _____ billion.

   six

2. _____ is the term for the scientific study of population statistics.

   Demography

3. The inability of an area to support its population due to the lack of certain environmental and ecological factors can lead to _____.

   overpopulation

4. About _____ percent of the people on Earth live on about _____ percent of the Earth's surface.

   seventy-five, five

5. Most of India's population live in cities or other _____ areas.

   urban

6. MDC stands for a _____ _____ _____.

   more developed country

7. _____ is the world's most populated country, though it will be replaced by _____ in the middle of the coming century due to a higher rate of natural increase.

   China, India

8. Seventy-five percent of Europeans live in _____ areas.

   urban

9. Ground that is permanently frozen is known as _____ and is found in large areas in the high _____.

   permafrost, latitudes

10. The total number of people divided by the area of land in their region is its _____ _____.

    arithmetic density

11. Land suited for agriculture is called _____ land.

    arable

12. Density that measures the number of people per unit of arable land is called _____ density.

    physiological

13. The number of farmers per unit of arable land is called _____ density.

    agricultural

14. Most LDC's have _____ agricultural densities because their farming techniques are less efficient than methods employed by farmers in MDC's.

15. It is accepted that the first revolution of innovation for humankind began around _____ B.C..   8,000

16. The Agricultural Revolution brought about the domestication of _____ and _____ which was a more reliant supply of nutrition than the previous methods of hunting and gathering.   plants, animals

17. The Medical Revolution greatly reduced the crude _____ rates in many _____ developed countries.   death
less

18. The _____ revolution originated in England, bringing much wealth to the country because of new manufacturing techniques.   industrial

19. The rate of _____ _____ is the percentage of which a population grows each year.   natural increase

20. The total number of deaths for every 1,000 people in society is known as the _____ _____ _____.   crude death rate

21. The infant mortality rate measures the number of deaths among infants aged _____ _____ and younger.   one year

22. Demographic transition refers to the growth and dynamics that occur to the _____ of countries as the evolve form less developed countries into more developed countries.   populations

23. During Stage 1 of demographic transition there are _____ growth rates, and at Stage 4 of the demographic transition there are _____ growth rates.   low
low

24. The nations of Sweden, Germany, and the United Kingdom have entered stage _____ of demographic transition.   four

25. Economic changes in stage _____ induce people to have fewer babies than in the two previous stages.   three

26. When the crude death rate and crude birth rate become equal, _____ _____ _____ occurs.   zero population growth

27. _____ is a good model for demographic transition because it has not changed its boundaries much nor has it been affected by migration significantly, and it has a good deal of population data available for the past millennia.   England

28. Population pyramids measure the break down of population by _____ and _____.

gender, age

29. A population pyramid with a very wide base and a narrow top represent the populations in _____ developed countries.

less

30. The number of people who don't work in a society compared to the number of people who are in their working years is known as the _____ _____.

dependency ratio

31. Gender-wise, slightly _____ males than females are born.

more

32. In the U.S. and Europe, there are about _____ men alive for every _____ women.

95
100

33. Since the 1950's the island nation of _____ _____ has remained in the Stage 2 of demographic transition.

Cape Verde

34. The English economist _____ _____, wrote the controversial work, An Essay on the Principle of Population, which theorized _____ growth would rise faster than the technology can supply it with food.

Thomas Malthus

population

35. Contemporary analysts who support Malthus are known as _____-_____.

Neo-Malthusians

36. Improving the educational status of women will serve to _____ the rate of natural increase in LDC's.

lower

37. The one-child policy has been employed by the government of _____ to reduce rates of natural increase in that country.

China

38. By the middle of the twenty-first century, _____ will surpass _____ as the world's most populous country.

India
China

CHAPTER THREE

MIGRATION

OVERVIEW

People have always moved from places they perceived to be of less desirability to more attractive places. Sometimes migrations are within a small region, while others bring emigrants around the world to new homelands. Some people are forced to move from their homes because governments see them as a threat, or simply as an annoyance. Push and pull factors are discussed in this chapter as well as examples of migrations that have happened in the world.

SELECTED NOTES

Migrating in Somalia (100): Due to drought and civil war, many people in the East African country of Somalia were forced by hunger to move from their home areas in order to survive. One such family was the Omer family, which was forced to move from their farm in rural Somalia (after three of their children died from starvation because of livestock theft and crop failings) to a camp where international relief agencies were thought to be dispensing food. The parents and three remaining children survived through 1992 and 1993, though approximately 300,000 Somalis perished from famine and warfare in 1992.

Migration and Emigration (101): The movement of people across the landscape from one place to another is called *mobility*. Spreading ideas and concepts as people move about the landscape is *relocation diffusion*. With modern communications and transportation, ideas and concepts spread rapidly through the world; that spread is called *expansive diffusion*. *Diffusion* is the process by which a characteristic disseminates over the landscape. When people move from one place to another in a "permanent" fashion it is called *migration*. People migrate for economic, political, climatic, and other reasons when oppression or opportunity are presented. Migration is divided into *emigration* and *immigration*. Emigrants are people leaving a country, while immigrants are people who arrive at a new country. So, if a family moves from Jamaica to Canada, they begin their journey as emigrants from Jamaica and eventually arrive in Canada as immigrants. The numerical difference between the total number of immigrants and emigrants is *net migration*. A positive net migration means the region has *net in-migration,* while a negative net-migration is a *net out-migration*.

Push Factors (101-104): Factors that cause people to leave a place are known as push factors. Push factors are divided into three categories: *1-Political, 2-Economic, and 3-Environmental*. People who are forced out of their country or region for political reasons are called *refugees*. When the former Soviet Union invaded Afghanistan in 1979, more than five million Afghans eventually left the country due to political oppression. In the U.S., many Cubans have came to southern Florida for what they believed were political push factors. If a person's native country affords little economic opportunity, migration to a country with "greener pastures" often occurs. These incentives for migration are called economic push factors. Many of the Irish who immigrated to the U.S. in the nineteenth century did so because of the failed potato crop, which brought famine and hardship to Ireland. Adverse environmental conditions often push people from their homes. When water is over-abundant (flooding) or is not present for human nourishment and irrigation, people are often pushed from their homelands. When people live on flood plains they are often eventually pushed out because of flooding disasters that wreck their homes and livelihoods. On the other hand, lack of rain, drought, also causes migration. In the 1930's, prolonged drought in the states of the southern Great Plains initiated the mass migration to California. Such migrants were called "**Okies.**"

Pull Factors (104-106): As with push factors, pull factors are classified as either: *1-Political, 2-Economic, or 3-Environmental.* Pull factors are positive features of a foreign land that lure people to migrate. The major political pull factor is political freedom that may exist in a country other than where the potential migrant is in residence. Often, when people live in a repressed, totalitarian country, the existence of a democratic republic which offers many more political freedoms pulls them toward it. The opportunity to increase the living standards of one's family often brings people to migrate to lands of greater economic opportunity. This is the primary reason for people to migrate to the U.S. and Canada. When Mexicans and other Latin Americans migrate to the U.S. in legal or illegal channels it is most often for jobs that will pay them more than they received in their native countries. The amenities offered by an area's environment often serve to pull people into those regions. For example, the beauty and recreational activities offered by the state of Colorado have lured many people to live there. Ironically, the mass migrations of recent years have produced pollution, which is what originally pushed many current residents to this destination. Many elderly people have moved to the warm climates of Arizona and Florida, where ailments associated with aged persons are less aggravating.

Intervening Obstacle (106): Migrants who are lured to a new location are often restricted from traveling to that location due to *intervening obstacles*. Mostly, these are physical barriers which prevent the passage of human beings and their desired belongings to a particular area. For example, the Atlantic Ocean, Rocky Mountains, Great Plains, and many other formidable physical obstacles effectively blocked many migrants from completing their journeys to new lands. However, such obstacles may be human-made; the Berlin Wall, which was erected to prevent migration to the West by Eastern Bloc people, was a recent example.

International and Internal Migration (106-109): *International migration* is the move from one country to another, while *internal migration* is the journey from one place to another area within the same country. *Voluntary migration* means that people have migrated due to their own free will, usually for economic improvement; *forced migration* means that a migrant has been compelled to move.

European Immigration to the U.S. (109): In the 500 years since Columbus sailed from Spain to the New World, about *60 million* Europeans have migrated to other continents, representing the world's largest migration. After 1800, huge population growth engulfed Europe as it moved into *Stage 2* of the demographic transition. This pushed many people to come to North America, southern South America, Australia and New Zealand, where climates and soils were similar, and, therefore, more familiar. Some Europeans did settle in tropical climates, but mostly for administrational purposes. In plantation areas in Latin America and Asia, most of the workers were natives or African slaves forcefully brought to the new lands.

Waves of Immigration from Europe to the United States (109-111): Of the 60 million European immigrants since 1500, *37 million* settled in the United States. *Germany* was the largest supplier of immigrants, followed by Italy, Great Britain, Ireland, Austria-Hungary, and Russia. From the first permanent colony in the U.S. in *Jamestown, Virginia* in 1607 until 1840 a steady stream of immigrants landed in what is now the United States' east coast. By the 1840's and 1850's immigration was annually over a quarter million people as the *first peak* of European migration was experienced. During these two decades, more people immigrated to the United States than in the previous 250 years. The immigrants of this time, as a whole, originated in northern and western Europe, from Ireland to Germany. Better incomes and standard of livings propelled these and future migrants. As the 1880's passed, the U.S. experienced a *second peak* of European immigration, again with most of the immigrants beginning their journeys in northern and western Europe. These people had ventured to America primarily because of available land that was relatively scarce in their homelands. The late 1890's and first fifteen years of the twentieth century witnessed the *third peak* of European immigration. However, this wave originated from Italy, Russia, and Austria-Hungary (which then included much of eastern Europe). This shift in source coincided with the industrial revolution's proceeding to these areas, leading them to later stages in the demographic transition.

Impact of European Migration (111-112): The dispersion throughout the world of 60 million Europeans has greatly altered the world's cultural landscape. Because of this population out-migration, Indo-European languages are spoken by half the world's population, Christianity reigns as the most popular religion on the globe, and European-inspired cultures and governments dominate in parts of Asia, Africa, and most of the New World, where, 500 years ago, they were completely absent. Economies in Africa and Asia were constructed by Europeans to supply raw materials to their homeland colonial powers.

Changes in U.S. Immigration Policy (112): Massive European migration to the U.S. ended with the onset of World War I. Ever since, the numbers of European immigrants has steadily dwindled. By the 1960's, only one-third of immigrants were from Europe and, since 1980, less than ten percent have been. During this steady decline in migration, European rates of natural increase have stabilized nearly to a static point.

Changing Attitudes & Quotas (112-113): By 1912, all of what is now the coterminous U.S. had been officially established as states. Consequently, many "Americans" believed that the arrival of more immigrants would just increase the competition for land and jobs. Many people believed there was no longer available land and jobs for more immigrants, who would strain the economy. During the third peak in immigration (when immigration sources shifted to southern and eastern Europe) established Americans often became hostile toward the new immigrants who had different origins than previous arrivals. The appearance of a handful of Japanese and Chinese immigrants led many Americans become paranoid about the possibility a huge influx of Asians into the country. Eventually, antagonism toward immigrants lead to the establishment of quotas in the forms of the *Quota Act of 1921* and the *National Origins Act of 1924*. *Quotas* in this context are the maximum number of people allowed entry into the U.S. in a given year. These quotas allowed for two percent of the existing ethnicity of the population of the U.S. to be allowed to immigrate each year according to the 1910 Census. This procedure served to perpetuate the base of the existing population, shaped by previous immigrants. Thus, immigrants from the Eastern Hemisphere were restricted to Europe. By the 1960's, such narrowly focused laws were replaced by statutes which allowed for no more than 290,000 immigrants each year, with no country allowing more than 20,000 emigrants access to the U.S. annually. In 1990, the global quota was set at 714,000 per year and in 1995 it is 675,000. Due to the high demand of applicants seeking to reside in the U.S., Congress has given preferential status to those immigrants who have established family members living in the U.S..

Impact of Quota Laws (113-114): After immigration laws were changed in the 1960's, the composition of incoming immigrants shifted from a mostly European blend to a mixture dominated by Latin Americans and Asians. Today, five-sixths of all immigrants to the U.S. come from these two regions. Contemporary leaders in U.S. immigrants are Mexico, Jamaica, Haiti, and the Dominican Republic. Asians have taken advantage of the U.S. immigration statutes by establishing one relative who, over time, helps bring relatives into the U.S.. Asians also tend to represent higher percentages of immigrants in Canada than in the U.S.. Such practices are known as **chain migration**. Many migrants come to the U.S. because their high levels of education promise them a good living. When a large exodus of highly educated professionals leave a LDC for an MDC such as the U.S., it is known as **brain drain**. Ultimately, most immigrants who reach the U.S., do so to improve their economic status.

Undocumented U.S. Immigration (114-118): Because demand for entry into the U.S. exceeds the number of slots opened by the American government, many people enter the country as *undocumented immigrants* who possess neither the permission of the government to enter nor official documents certifying the lawful entry of such persons. Three-fourths of the undocumented immigrants who enter the U.S. every year, come from a Latin American country. Half of all illegal immigrants cross the international frontier illegally while the other half simply remain here after their work or student visas expire. Most undocumented immigrants from Mexico are young males between the ages of fifteen and thirty-four who leave their families and villages in Mexico to work in the U.S., and systematically send portions of their earnings home to Mexico. Crossing the U.S.-Mexico border is not a difficult task, given its 2,000 mile length through sparsely populated desert. Once a group of Mexicans enter the U.S., they contact someone known as a *coyote* who brings them to a city within the U.S., where they hopefully are able to find employment. Often the *U.S. Border Patrol* intercepts illegal immigrants and routinely deports them to border cities in Mexico, where they promptly attempt to cross the border again. During the 1990's, the state of California, at the urging of its citizens, enacted legislation to deny public access to illegal immigrants.

Guest Workers (118-120): Millions of people come to the Middle East and Western Europe to work. In these cases the migrants are known as *guest workers*. Guest workers take low-status and low-income jobs that local residents don't want, as do many undocumented immigrants in the U.S.. In Europe, guest workers are protected by minimum wage laws and labor union contracts. In Switzerland and Luxembourg, guest workers exceed ten percent of the population, while in Germany, Belgium, and France they constitute over five percent of the population. European guest workers originate in North Africa, Eastern Europe, the Middle East, and Asia. Since the fall of communism in formerly East Bloc countries, more guest workers have came from Eastern Europe to Western Europe in search of employment. Although guest worker arrangements are suppose to be temporary, many become permanent residents of the host country. In recent years as economic growth has slowed in Middle Eastern and Western European countries, so has the willingness of these countries to accept guest workers. Attacks upon immigrants in Europe have escalated in recent years. The United Kingdom severely restricts the number of work permits given to foreigners.

Migration in Asia (120): Asians have migrated in the millions to foreign lands to earn a living. Today there are 29 million ethnic Chinese living abroad, mostly in Asia. Chinese immigrants helped to build the first transcontinental railroad in the U.S., completed in 1869. Indians have also migrated to places like Burma, Malaysia, Guyana in South America, and South Africa. Indians also emigrated to the island of Fiji; political problems have arisen since they now outnumber the native Fijian population. Japanese have moved to South America and Hawaii.

Migrations Between Regions Within the United States (120-124): *Interregional migration* is the movement from one region of a country to another, while *intraregional migration* is the movement within one area. The settlement of the American West is the most famous example of large-scale internal migration. Through this migration, the sparse interior of the U.S. was settled. Since the first U.S. Census was taken in 1790, the geographic center of the U.S. population has been steadily moving westward, and in recent years a few degrees of latitude southward. This migration indicates the changing preference for living in the Western and Southern U.S.. The population center moved very fast between 1830 and 1880, when mass migration was bringing people to California during the gold rush. Railroads and barbed wire helped pioneers to settle the Great Plains. After 1880, the population center still shifted westward, but much slower. Since 1950, the population has again been moving rapidly South and West because population has been drawn to these regions for economic and environmental (climatic) reasons.

Internal African-American Migration (124-125): A hundred years ago, most African-Americans lived in the South, where their ancestors were forcefully brought as slaves earlier in history. However, during this century many migrated northward to cities in the Northeast, Midwest, and West. Migrants to each of these disconnected areas tended to have distinct geographic roots in the South.

Interregional Migration in Other Countries (125-127): In the *Soviet Union* there were excellent sources of raw materials located in isolated parts of Russia. In order to develop fully those resources the government encouraged migration within the country by offering higher pay than in other regions. However, the remoteness and harsh, frigid climate of the northern reaches of the country drove most of the workers of the Far North to more hospitable areas. *Brazil* desired very much to move some of its population move to the interior of the country, with the objective of developing unexploited resources in the inner continental areas of Brazil. A new capitol, Brasilia, was constructed in the interior in the 1950's. However, most migrants could not afford the housing and ultimately lived in shanty towns known as "favelas" on the outskirts of the city. *Indonesia* has attempted to decentralize the core of its population on the island of Java to less populated islands. Incentives given by the government included land and materials to begin farming. In *Europe*, different levels of income have induced people to move from poorer areas to more lucrative ones. For example, in *Italy* the poor southern Italians often migrate to northern Italy where incomes are nearly double that of the southern *Mezzogiorno,* and has a quarter of its unemployment. The *Assam* region of *India* is protected from immigrants so that the way of life will not become dominated by new migrants. A permit is needed by anyone wishing to visit or migrate to Assam.

Intraregional Migration (127-129): People more often move to another location within their original region in the form of *intraregional migration*. Most often in the last two hundred years this has occurred as *rural to urban migration*. For example, the urban population of the U.S. increased from five percent in 1800 to fifty percent by 1920. Rural to urban migration has become very intense in recent years in Africa, Latin America, and Asia. Often, as in the case of the Brazilian city of Sao Paulo the cities cannot accommodate the new arrivals who are forced by lack of space to live in squatter towns called *"favelas"*. In MDC's the intraregional trend is from the *city cores into the suburbs*. The suburbs lure people because of lower crime rates, larger homes, more green space, more recreational amenities, and less congestion. Since the 1970's MDC's in Europe and North America have witnessed a swing in intraregional migration from *metropolitan areas to rural areas*. This phenomena is titled *counterurbanization*. Like suburbanization, people move to rural areas from cities for lifestyle reasons. With cheap modern communication and transportation, living in more isolated locations is not as unproductive as in the past. Retirees constitute a part of these migrants. In the U.S. counterurbanization has slowed since the early 1980's because jobs have declined in these areas. Worsening agricultural conditions have also decreased the allure of the countryside.

Slavery Forces International Migration (130-131): In order to develop the economies of the New World, Europeans began importing Africans. At least *ten million Africans* were eventually uprooted and taken to work in the western hemisphere where abundant and cheap labor was needed. Slaves were mainly sent to the islands of the Caribbean, Brazil, and the United States. The extraction from villages in Africa of the youngest and strongest members obviously had negative ramifications upon the long term life of the communities. Twenty-five percent of the African slaves died on the ships bringing them to the New World. The *triangular trade* was a system whereby slaves, rum, sugar, and molasses would be exchanged between the U.S., the Caribbean, and the United Kingdom. *Australia* was first settled by convicts from the United Kingdom. By the middle 1800's 165,000 convicts had been deported to Australia. Many convicts decided to settle there after their sentences were served.

War Forces International Migration (131-135): World War I caused six million people to migrate internationally while World War II, forced forty-five million people to move across international borders. World War II migrations were caused mainly by the expansion of the German and Japanese armies. In Africa, there have been wars in the four Horn nations of Eritrea, Ethiopia, Somalia, and Sudan which have initiated migrations. The Eritreans saw themselves as an independent nation within Ethiopia, but were not recognized by that nation. Thus, differences in territorial opinion lead to war between these states, leading 665,000 Eritreans to seek refuge in Sudan. However, Eritrea became an autonomous state in 1993. Ethiopia also warred with Somalia, dislodging 365,000 Ethiopians of Somalian descent. Meanwhile, internal civil war in Somalia in recent years has produced hundreds of thousands of refugees. In Rwanda, 3.4 million people were either killed or became refugees in neighboring countries when civil war erupted between the Tutsi's and Hutu's, its two dominant ethnic groups. In East Africa, Mozambique was the scene of a civil war in 1976 which produced 1.4 million refugees. The African refugees are often in shockingly poor physical condition, due to chronic lack of food and water.

India and Pakistan (135-136): When Great Britain ended colonial rule in South Asia, the sub-continent was divided into two countries based upon religious affiliation. Pakistan was chiefly Muslim while India was dominated by Hindus. In order to homogenize the populations of each country into a more uniformly religious one, Hindus from Pakistan migrated to India while Muslims from India moved to Pakistan. During these mass migrations that found 17 million people moving due to their religious affiliations, opposing radical groups often killed emigrants in transit. Conflict between India and Pakistan continues today, because of perceptual differences in the boundary between the two nations. In 1973, Pakistan itself had a civil war in which Eastern Pakistan broke off to form an independent country which is known today as Bangladesh.

Ethnic Cleansing in Former Yugoslavia (136-137): In the 1990's, Yugoslavia was divided into independent states whose boundaries were supposed to correspond to ethnic populations. However, two million people were forced to move from areas where they were the minority. This process is called *ethnic cleansing*. Many journalists have reported that Serbs have often performed ethnic cleansing against the Muslims of the former Yugoslavia. Often the Muslims have been killed when they resist Serbian aggression. Muslims are divided into groups of potential troublemakers (able-bodied men) and non-threatening groups (mainly women and children).

Government Ideology Forces Migrations (137): When different governments have come into power throughout history, it is not uncommon for them to force groups that are either threatening or undesirable to leave the country. After World War II, the Communist government of *Bulgaria* forced one million ethnic Turks from the country, and banned the Turkish language and their religious rites. After the 1959 revolution in *Cuba,* 700,000 Cubans fled the country due to ideological differences with the new communist government. In 1980 another large wave of 125,000 Cubans migrated to the U.S. in one program (Mariel Boatlift). The U.S. was ill-prepared to handle such large numbers of refugees, and had to accommodate them for a time in tents and in the Orange Bowl. Soon after the Mariel Boatlift, thousands of Haitians came to the U.S. seeking a new homeland. After proving that their reasons for migration were political rather than economic, the Haitians were allowed to stay in the U.S..

Changing U.S. Policies Toward Immigration (137-138): Until the early twentieth century the U.S. welcomed immigrants with open arms, for they were a valuable factor in developing the country's economy. However, the middle and later parts of the twentieth century brought more skeptical attitudes towards immigrants who found immigration to the U.S. more difficult than in previous times. The tradition of universal immigration to the U.S. and Canada has dwindled greatly during the last third of the twentieth century.

Migration Transition (139-141): These are a series of migration changes that concur with the stages of the demographic transition. During the first stage of the demographic transition, few migrations occur. However, in the second stage with high population growth, people move to the cities from the country, and people emigrate to other countries where populations stress those nations less than the country of origin. In stages three and four, fewer people tend to migrate abroad, however, there is significant intraregional migration when people move from city cores to the suburban areas more distant from urban areas. As more countries enter the third and fourth stages of demographic transition, their countries will look for immigrants to supplement their sagging or declining populations.

CLOSING REMARKS

People migrate due to push and pull factors. Motivations to migrate stem from economic, political, and environmental reasons. When people migrate interregionally or intraregionally, it is to improve their perceived quality of life. This statement holds true for people who move from country to country or from the city core into the suburbs. Forced migration is often borne of political urgings. As more MDC's enter the fourth stage of the demographic transition, it will be interesting to note the migration increases that may occur to supplement some of their stability populations.

KEY TERMS AND CONCEPTS

Mobility: The ability to move from one location to another. Mobility may be hindered by physical barriers such as deserts, mountains, and bodies of water.

Migration: Form of relocation diffusion involving a permanent move to a new location. The entire journey made by a person or group of persons.

Emigration: Migration from a location. When people leave a country, they emigrate.

Immigration: Migration to a new location. When people arrive in a new country, they have immigrated.

Net-Migration: The difference between the level of immigration and the level of emigration. This variable, along with rates of natural increase, determines population growth.

Push Factors: Factors that induced people to leave their former residences. Poor political, economic, and environmental conditions in one's native country often cause people to emigrate.

Pull Factors: Factors that induce people to move to a new location. Increased political freedom and more lucrative jobs often pull people into other, more promising countries.

Refugees: People who are forced to migrate from a country for political reasons. Recently, the U.S. has harbored refugees from China, Haiti, Cuba, Vietnam and many other countries.

Flood Plain: The area subject to flooding during a given number of years according to historical trends. Flood plains often have large populations that suffer greatly when flooding occurs at disastrous levels.

Intervening Obstacles: An environmental or cultural feature of the landscape that hinders migration. The Berlin Wall, border patrols, border fences, and customs officers are all cultural intervening obstacles.

International Migration: Permanent movement from one country to another. During the 1800's many people from Europe migrated to the U.S. and Canada.

Internal Migration: Permanent movement within a particular country. When the people of the southern plains, "Okies", migrated to California during the Dust Bowl of the 1930's, they were internally migrating.

Voluntary Migration: Permanent movement undertaken by choice. In this case, the migrants moved for no politically-forced reason.

Forced Migration: Permanent movement compelled usually by political factors. People whom the government in power perceive as threatening or undesirable are frequently forced to migrate.

Guest Workers: Workers who migrate to the more developed countries of Northern and Western Europe, (usually from southern or Eastern Europe, or from northern Africa), in search of higher paying jobs. Guest workers fill a niche of jobs that are often left unattended by the people in the host country.

Quota: In reference to migration, a law that places maximum limits on the number of people who can immigrate to a country. Today, the quota for immigrants to the U.S. is 20,000 per country of origin.

Chain Migration: A process by which people are given preference for migrating to another country because a relative was previously admitted. Asians are known to be effective users of chain migration.

Brain Drain: Large-scale emigration by talented people. LDC's complain that their more talented people often migrate to MDC's such as the U.S. due to better paying jobs.

Undocumented Immigrants: People who illegally enter the U.S. to live and work. There is much debate concerning the benefits and disadvantages of illegal immigrants upon the U.S. economy.

Interregional Migration: Permanent movement from one region of a country to another. In the U.S., elderly people commonly move from cold regions to the warmer climates of the Southwest or Southeast.

Intraregional Migration: Permanent movement within one region of a country. This can be the movement from rural hinterlands to cities, or the migration from city cores to the suburbs.

Counterurbanization: Net migration from urban to rural areas. People move to small towns and rural areas, due to better communications and the lure of cleaner and more peaceful surroundings.

Triangular Slave Trade: A practice, primarily during the eighteenth century, of European ships transporting slaves form Africa to Caribbean islands, molasses from the Caribbean to Europe, and trade goods from Europe to Africa.

Ethnic Cleansing: The process by which a more powerful ethnic group forcibly relocates a less powerful one, so that the more powerful group can be the sole inhabitants of a region. In this century this has been practiced by Turks against Armenians, Nazi's against Jews and Slavs, and by Serbs against Muslims.

Migration Transition: Change in the migration pattern in a society that results from industrialization, population growth, and other social and economic changes that also produce the demographic transition. It corresponds to stages in the demographic transition.

1. The ability of humans to move from one place to another is known as _____.

mobility

2. Migration is the _____ move by people from one place to another.

permanent

3. Negative perceptions of the political, economic, and environmental conditions of their own countries that induce people to move are called _____ _____.

push factors

4. Pull factors are conditions which induce people to _____ to a new location.

move

5. The three major types of push factors are _____, _____, and _____.

political, economic, environmental

6. The largest number of refugees in the world was a result of the Soviet Union's invasion of _____.

Afghanistan

7. Most Afghan refugees sought refuge in the countries of _____ and _____.

Pakistan
Iran

8. Several million Irish were pushed from their homeland due to the destruction of their _____ crop by a fungus.

potato

9. The Dust Bowl of the 1930's pushed "Okies" to migrate; They moved primarily to the state of _____.

California

10. The most important pull factor for immigrants to the U.S. and Canada is _____ _____.

economic improvement

11. In the U.S., the state of _____ has pulled many people to it because of the climate's reputation for low pollen counts.

Arizona

12. The Atlantic Ocean, Rocky Mountains, and Sahara have acted as _____ _____ to people who wanted to migrate across them.

intervening obstacles

13. International migration is the permanent movement of people from one _____ to another.

country

14. _____ migration is where migrants have been compelled to emigrate from a country due to political factors.

Forced

15. In the past 500 years, about _____ million people have left Europe for new lives on other continents.

60

16. The largest supplier of emigrants to the United States from Europe has been _____, with 7.1 million.

Germany

17. Ninety percent of the immigrants to the U.S. before 1840, originated in _____ _____.

Great Britain

18. The first two peaks of European immigration to the U.S. came from _____ and _____ Europe.

Northern, Western

19. Arizona and _____ _____ were the last two of the contiguous forty-eight states to be admitted.

New Mexico

20. In 1921, the U.S. set _____ to curb the number of immigrants in the U.S..

quotas

21. The U.S. yearly issues _____ visas to legal immigrants.

675,000

22. _____ drain is the exodus of talented people from an LDC due to more lucrative job offers elsewhere.

Brain

23. Since the 1960's, five-sixths of all immigrants come from Latin America and _____.

Asia

24. People who arrive in the U.S. without the consent of the U.S. government are called _____ _____.

undocumented immigrants

25. A person who, for a price, helps Mexicans enter the U.S. illegally is called a _____.

coyote

26. The border between the U.S. and _____ extends over 2,000 miles, and is witness to a large amount of illegal immigration.

Mexico

27. People who migrate to Europe and Middle Eastern countries to work, but do not receive citizenship are known as _____ _____.

guest workers

28. The _____ _____ receives many immigrants from countries that are its former colonies.

United Kingdom

29. A person who moves from one place to another within the same region is practicing _____ _____. intraregional migration

30. Since the 1790 U.S. Census, the geographic center of the U.S. population has continually moved mostly _____ and slightly _____ of its original position. West, South

31. During the last one-hundred years, African-Americans in the U.S. have migrated from the _____ to northern cities such as New York, Detroit, and Chicago. South

32. _____ constructed a new capitol in the interior of the country to facilitate settlement of the interior. Brazil

33. Migration from rural to _____ areas has skyrocketed in recent years in Asia, Latin America, and Africa. urban

34. Australia was settled originally by _____. convicts

35. Eritrea was engaged in conflict with _____ before it became an independent state in 1993. Ethiopia

36. Serbs have been accused of performing _____ _____ upon Bosnian Muslims in the former Yugoslavia. ethnic cleansing

37. The Mariel Boatlift brought emigrants from _____ to the U.S.. Cuba

CHAPTER FOUR

LANGUAGES

OVERVIEW

Languages are integral to people, enabling them to converse with one another. Language is a component of culture and individual identity. English is a particularly interesting case study because of its familiarity to the reader. Having an extensive written history, there is much to examine to understand the evolution of English through time. All languages change and evolve with the peoples who use them. Moving from place to place, country to country, or continent to continent, people take their languages with them. New languages evolve from the marriage of cultures. Today, English is spoken around the world. It is spoken differently in America, England, South Africa, India, and a multitude of other places because each place has had different influences. Americans have lived in relative isolation from England, allowing the two to evolve differently. The same is true of cultures and languages around the world, giving rise to unique language families, branches, groups, and dialects.

SELECTED NOTES

Language (149): *Language* is a system of communication through speech, a collection of sounds that a group of people understands to have the same meaning. The written version of a language is called a *literary tradition,* which may or may not exist alongside the *verbal language*, or a spoken language. Languages are related to one another and can be described by their family, branch, group, and dialect. A *language family* includes individual languages related through a common ancestor that existed before recorded history. The Indo-European family contains 50% of the world's population, Sino-Tibetan contains 20 %, and 20% in four families–Austronesian, Afro-Asiatic, Niger-Congo, and Dravidian. The remaining 10% of the population speaks a variety of other languages. A *language branch* includes tongues that share a common origin but have further evolved into individual languages. A *language group* comprises individual languages within a branch that share a common origin in the relatively recent past and display relatively few differences in grammar and vocabulary. A *dialect* is a form of a language spoken in a local area. The *standard language* is the dialect of a language which is used for government, business, education, and mass communication.

Development of English (149-153): Language *originates* in a given place and *diffuses* through migration of its speakers. English is a conglomeration of many languages. Very little is known about the original occupants of the British Isles. The Celts arrived about

2000 B.C. and spoke Celtic. In 450 A.D. the Angles from southern Denmark, the Jutes from northwestern Germany, and the Saxons from northwestern Germany all brought the *Germanic dialects* which are the basis for English. Being a **Germanic language**, English shares many words and has structural similarities with other Germanic languages. The *Viking* invasion from the 800's contributed words to English when they remained and were absorbed into the culture. The *Norman French* conquered England in 1066 and established French as the **official language** for the next 150 years, though the majority of people continued to speak English. An **official language** is a language adopted for use by the government. In 1204 King John lost control of Normandy, and English became the preferred language. In 1362 Parliament passed the Statute of Pleading, making English the official language. English was diffused around the world through colonization. The first British colonies were founded in North America, followed by South America, Africa, Asia, and islands in the Atlantic, Indian, and Pacific oceans. Many colonies used English as the official language, even while the majority spoke another language. With independence, many of the former colonies established indigenous languages as the official language. Many countries used (and still use) English to conduct international communication. Familiarity with English has made it a **lingua franca**, a language used in commerce by people who have different native languages. Pidgin languages have evolved to enable communication, though they have no native speakers and are spoken in addition to a native language. A **pidgin language** is a language constructed by learning a few of the grammar rules and words of a lingua franca, while mixing in some elements of their own languages.

Other Germanic Languages (153-154): The original **Germanic** language has been lost as people have migrated and lived in relative isolation from one another, allowing their language to evolve independently. The common origin can be reconstructed by looking at language differences and similarities, among different languages in a group.

West Germanic Group: English and German (154): The **West Germanic group** is subdivided into *High* and *Low Germanic*, based on altitude. *High Germanic* is from the southern mountains of Germany and is the basis for modern standard *German*. *Low Germanic*, from northern Germany, was the home of the Angles, Jutes, and Saxons, thereby making *English* a Low Germanic language. *Old Saxon* was spoken by the Saxons who remained in the lowlands and evolved into *Low German*, a modern dialect of German. *Old Franconian* became *Dutch* and *Flemish* of the Netherlands and northern Belgium. *Old Frisian* became modern *Frisian*, spoken in the northeastern Netherlands by a few people.

North Germanic Group: Scandinavian Languages (154-155): **Old Norse** was the original language of Scandinavia. *Swedish, Danish, Norwegian,* and *Icelandic* evolved through isolation and political organization. Icelandic has remained essentially isolated since settlement by Norwegians in 874 A.D. making the language and its literary tradition extremely interesting for study.

Extinct East Germanic Group (155-156): This language group is now extinct. An *extinct language* is one which is no longer spoken or read in daily activities by anyone in the world. *Gothic* was spoken in eastern and northern Europe in the third century A.D. The last speaker died in the Crimea region of Russia in the sixteenth century. Its speakers were converted to other languages through integration.

Romance Language Branch: Latin and the Roman Empire (156-157): The ***Romance language branch*** evolved from the Latin language spoken by the ancient Romans. The Roman Empire reached its height in the second century A.D., and stretched from the Atlantic to the Black Sea and across the Mediterranean Sea. The Roman armies occupied the area, brought with them their language, and suppressed or extinguished the other languages. The Roman Empire grew over several hundred years, and the Latin spoken in a given area was that which was spoken by the army at that time. Variations arose due to time, and the integration of different words from the languages of the different provinces. ***Vulgar Latin,*** the form of Latin spoken by "the masses" of the populace, was the version spoken by the soldiers and transmitted to the provinces. When the Roman Empire collapsed in the fifth century, the various provinces were isolated from one another and different languages evolved.

Modern Romance Languages (158-159): The four most widely used ***modern Romance languages*** are *Spanish, Portuguese, French,* and *Italian.* The four languages roughly correspond to the countries *Spain, Portugal, France,* and *Italy* and were separated from one another by ***intervening obstacles.*** *Romanian* is the fifth most important Romance language and is spoken in *Romania* and *Moldova,* while being separated from other Romance-speaking countries by Slavic-speaking peoples. Many dialects exist within each province. The languages evolved slowly, and it is only recently that language has been standardized with a ***standard national language.*** Local differences tend to diminish or to disappear with the dominance of one dialect for political, economic, and social life.

Worldwide Diffusion of Spanish and Portuguese (159): Spanish and Portuguese have diffused to North, Central, and South America. Approximately 90% of the speakers of these languages live in the Americas. The languages were brought by the Spaniards and Portuguese who settled and explored the Americas. As in the case with English, Spanish and Portuguese evolved in the Americas in ways different from the ways they evolved in their places of origin. Portugal, Brazil, and several countries in Africa have all agreed to standardize the Portuguese language in order to increase interaction between these large and diverse groups of people.

How Many Romance Languages Exist? (159-162): Other Romance languages exist, though not to the same extent as the aforementioned. There are two other official Romance languages: *Romansh* of *Switzerland* with 25,000 speakers and *Catalan,* of *Andorra* with 50,000 speakers and the Spanish dialect spoken around *Barcelona* with another 9 million speakers. *Sardinian,* a mixture of Italian, Spanish and Arabic, was once the official language of the Mediterranean island of *Sardinia.* Unofficial languages include: *Ladin* of *Italy* with 20,000 speakers in the South Tyrol and *Friulian* of the northeast with 50,000 speakers. These two and *Romansh* are dialects of *Rhaeto-Romanic*. *Ladino* is a mixture of Spanish, Greek, Turkish and Hebrew and is spoken by 140,000 *Sephardic Jews*, most of whom now live in *Israel*. *Occitan* is a dialect of French, spoken in the former region of *Aquitaine*. These unofficial languages are all used in literature. There is a fine line between two languages' being separate dialects, or two distinct languages. Flemish of northern Belgium is considered by some a dialect and by others a separate language. The same is true of Galician of northwestern Spain and its relationship to Portuguese.

Creolized Languages (162): A ***creole*** or ***creolized language*** is one that results from the mixing of the colonizer's language with the indigenous language of the people being dominated. A creolized language forms when the colonized group adopts the language of the dominant group but makes some changes, such as simplifying the grammar and adding words from their former language. A creolized language evolves from a pidgin language to become the primary language of a cultural group. As it does so, the creole language needs to expand greatly its vocabulary. *French Creole* spoken in *Haiti* and *Portuguese Creole* of the *Cape Verde Islands* are good examples.

Indic (Eastern) Group of Indo-Iranian Language Branch (163): ***Indic languages*** are the second largest language group in the world. This branch encompasses the most widely used languages of India, Pakistan, and Bangladesh. One third of *Indians* speak ***Hindi***, which can be spoken in many different ways though there is only one official way to write the language–using a script called ***Devanagari***. This script has been used since the seventh century A.D. The written language has remained consistent for all Hindi speakers, because very few people could read or write, maintaining the written language even while the spoken language changed in different locals. The ***Indo-Iranian branch*** has the most speakers of the languages of this family, including more than 100 individual languages and more than 1 billion people. *Pakistan* uses *Urdu* which is much like Hindi, though written using the ***Arabic alphabet***. Most Pakistanis are Muslims and the Quran is written in Arabic. ***Hindustani*** is the basis for both languages. Hindi was the dialect from New Delhi and was encouraged by the British for use in government in the nineteenth century. *Bengali* is spoken in *Bangladesh*, and *Punjabi, Marthi,* and *Gajariti* are Indic languages in *South Asia*. *India* became an independent state from England in 1947 and in 1950 established fourteen official languages–ten Indo-European (Assamese, Bengali, Gujarati, Hindi, Kashmiri, Marathi, Oriya, Punjabi, Sanskrit, and Urdu) and four Dravidian languages (Kannada, Malayalam, Tamil, and Telugu)–spoken by 90% of Indians, the remaining 10 million use other languages. English is an "associate" language though few can speak it. It is often employed by Indians who can't communicate in a common Indian tongue.

Iranian (Western) Group of Indo-Iranian Language Branch (163): The ***Iranian group*** of languages are spoken in Iran and neighboring countries in southwestern Asia. The main languages include *Persian* in *Iran*, *Pashto* in eastern *Afghanistan* and western *Pakistan* and *Kurdish* of the *Kurds* of western *Iran*, northern *Iraq*, and eastern *Turkey*. All are written with the ***Arabic alphabet***.

Balto-Slavic Language Branch of Indo-European (163): **Slavic** was the original language, branching off in the seventh century when Slavs migrated from Asia to Europe creating East, West, and South Slavic groups as well as a Baltic group. Slavic languages are not easily differentiated as differences are relatively small. They are generally mutually intelligible, though differences are a source of pride and are being preserved and in some cases accentuated in recent independence movements.

East Slavic and Baltic Groups of Balto-Slavic Language Branch (163-165): **Eastern Slavic languages** are the most widely used Slavic languages. Russian is one of the six official languages of the United Nations, as well as being the lingua franca for people of the former Soviet Union. More than 80% of Russians speak the language as well as many other peoples who were once part of the Soviet Union. Language was forced into use and taught as a second language to encourage unity. Language was a major force in the breakup of the Soviet Union. *Ukrainian* and *Belorusian* are the next most wide-spread East Slavic languages and have been established as the official languages in *Ukraine* and *Belarus*. The two principal Baltic languages are *Latvian* and *Lithuanian*, official languages of *Latvia* and *Lithuania*. *Estonian*, the official language of *Estonia*, is an **Uralic** language unrelated to the Indo-European family.

West and South Slavic Groups of Balto-Slavic Language Branch (165): *Polish*, followed by *Czech* and *Slovak,* are the mostcommonly spoken **Slavic languages**. During the Communist era, *Czechoslovakia* contained twice as many *Czechs* as *Slovaks* and tried to balance the use of the two languages, which are mutually understandable. In 1993 *Slovakia* ceded from the *Czech Republic*, renewing recurring feelings of resentment of perceived Czech dominance of the country's culture. **South Slavic** languages include *Serbo-Croatian* and *Bulgarian*. *Serbs* and *Croats* speak the same language; the former writing with the **Cyrillic alphabet** and the Croats using the **Roman alphabet**. *Slovene* is the official language of *Slovenia*, while *Macedonian* is used in the former *Yugoslav* republic of *Macedonia*.

Celtic Branch of Indo-European (165): Relatively few people speak languages from *other Indo-European branches: Albanian, Armenian, Celtic,* and *Greek*. **Celtic** is interesting for the English speaker. Two thousand years ago, Celtic languages were spoken in much of present-day Germany, France, and northern Italy, as well as the in the British Isles. These languages survive only in remote parts of *Scotland, Wales, Ireland,* and in the French region of *Brittany*.

Celtic Groups (165-167): There are two groups, *Goidelic* (Gaelic) and *Brythonic*. The two surviving Goidelic languages are *Irish Gaelic* with 75,000 exclusive speakers and *Scottish Gaelic* with 80,000 exclusive speakers. Irish Gaelic and English are the Republic of Ireland's two official languages. Gaelic has an extensive literary tradition. Speakers of *Brythonic* (also called Cymric or Britannic) fled to Wales, Cornwall, or to Brittany. The language which developed in Cornwall, *Cornish*, became **extinct** in 1777 when the last speaker died. In *Brittany*, 50,000 people still speak *Breton* which includes more French words. Language survival depends on the strength of its speakers. The Celts lost much territory and power to the Angles, Jutes, and Saxons. Increased transportation and communication has made English a necessity, decreasing Gaelic use in Wales, Scotland, and Ireland. Celtic Languages have enjoyed a recent resurgence. Welsh schools must teach the Welsh language, and folk history and music have been added to the curriculum. Road signs are posted in Welsh. The BBC produces Welsh-language programs. Folk and rock singers bring attention to the Gaelic languages. Cornish has been revived and now has several hundred speakers. It, too, is taught in grade schools and adult evening classes. The European Union has established the European Bureau of Lesser Used Languages, to help preserve about two dozen languages.

Search for the Indo-European Hearth (167): The search for the **Proto-Indo-European** hearth, or the original language of the Indo European branch, exemplifies the geographic principles of *area and spatial analysis, integrating cultural characteristics, region, diffusion,* and *distribution.*

Evidence of Common Origin of Indo-European Languages (167-168): Evidence of a common ancestor comes from the analysis of common words across the various languages. Common root words indicate "relatedness" between languages. Who were the people who formed the common connection in the origin of Indo-European languages?
Theory 1: Kurgan Origin: Marija Gimbutas proposed the Kurgan people of the steppes near the border between present-day Russia and Kazakhstan. These nomadic herders with horses conquered much of Europe and south Asia between 3500 and 2500 B.C.
Theory 2: Origin in Anatolia: Archaeologist Colin Renfrew proposes eastern Anatolia, part of modern Turkey, as the place of origin approximately 2,000 years before the Kurgans. He believes affluence from agricultural practices enabled growing prosperity to travel northward, eastward, westward, and either directly along the southern coasts of the Black and Caspian seas, or indirectly (by way of Russia), north of the seas.

A pre-Indo-European Survivor: Basque (169): The isolation of the Basques in the Pyrenees Mountains of northern Spain and southwestern France has helped preserve this pre-Indo-European language. Approximately 1 million people speak Basque. No attempt to link it to the Indo-European languages has been successful.

Asian Language Families (169-170): South Asian languages mostly fall into the Indo-European family. Other language families in Asia include **Sino-Tibetan, Japanese, Korean,** and **Southeast Asia** (all in east and southeast Asia), **Afro-Asiatic** (in southwest Asia, as well as northern Africa), and **Altaic** (in central Asia as well as Turkey).

Sino-Tibetan Language Family (170): The *People's Republic of China*–having over one billion people–and smaller countries in southeast Asia have languages in this family. China is mainly composed of the **Sinitic** branch. **Austro-Thai** and **Tibetan-Burman** are two smaller branches.

Sinitic Branch (170): There are several languages spoken in *China*, the most important is *Mandarin* spoken by 75% of the Chinese people. It is an official language of the United Nations and the official language of both the *People's Republic of China* and *Taiwan*. Four other Chinese languages are *Cantonese, Wu, Min*, and *Hakka*, though the government imposes Mandarin. All use a consistent written form, and the small number of languages contribute to a sense of unity. The Chinese languages are based on 420 one-syllable words, more different sounds than humans are able to make. Each actual spoken sound denotes more than one thing, and meaning is inferred from *context* in the sentence and the *tone of voice* used by the speaker. Multiple-syllable words are created which infer meaning. The 4,000 year old written language uses thousands of characters, some of which represent sounds. Most are ***ideograms*** which represent ideas or concepts rather than pronunciations.

Austro-Thai and Tibeto-Burman Branches of Sino-Tibetan Family (170-171): The major language of the ***Austro-Thai branch*** is *Thai*, used in *Laos, Thailand*, and parts of *Vietnam*. *Lao* is considered by some a separate language. The principal language of the ***Tibeto-Burman branch*** is *Burmese* used in *Myanmar*. The people of *Madagascar* migrated to the island approximately 2,000 years ago–apparently the Malayo-Polynesian people. Their closest language neighbor is 3,000 km away.

Japanese (171): The ***Japanese*** received their original writing system from the Chinese. The language structure differs. The Japanese use two systems of ***phonetic symbols*** either in place of the ideograms or alongside them.

Korean and Austro-Asiatic Language Families (171): ***Korean*** is classed separately though it is related to Japanese and the Altaic languages of central Asia. More than half the vocabulary is Chinese. Korean is written using ***hankul***, in which each letter represents a sound. ***Austro-Asiatic*** languages include *Vietnamese*, the dominant tongue of the Southeast Asian language family. It is written using the ***Latin alphabet,*** with many ***diacritical marks*** above the vowels. The system was developed in the seventh century by Roman Catholic missionaries.

Afro-Asiatic Language Family (171): This family includes Arabic and Hebrew and a number of languages spoken in northern Africa and southwestern Asia. It is the fourth largest language family. Languages of this family were used to write the holiest books of three world religions, the Judeo-Christian Bible and the Islamic Quran.

Arabic (171-172): ***Arabic*** is the dominant language of the Afro-Asiatic family with 200 million native speakers and numerous people familiar with it due to the Quran. Standard Arabic is based on the Quran, written in the seventh century. Newspapers, radio, and literature use standard Arabic. It is one of the official languages of the United Nations. Arabic usage spreads across countries in north Africa and southwest Asia.

Hebrew (172): ***Hebrew*** is a modern language revived after it died out in the fourth century. The Old Testament was written in Hebrew (a part was written in the Afro-

Asiatic language, *Aramaic*). Hebrew is the official language of *Israel*, a country created in 1948. The language is used to unite the Jewish population gathered from around the world. ***Eliezer Ben-Yehuda*** initiated the revival of Hebrew, creating words, writing the first modern Hebrew dictionary and refusing to speak any other language.

Altaic and Uralic Language Families (172): The two families are similar in word formation, grammatical endings, and other structural elements. They are believed to have separate origins. The ***Altaic family*** is thought to have come from the steppes bordering the Qilian Shan and Altai mountains between Tibet and China, or it may be a conglomeration of many languages which has evolved.

Altaic Languages (172-173): *Turkish* is the most widely spoken Altaic language. It is now written with the Latin alphabet, a change from Arabic ordered in 1928 by the Turkish government, led by *Kemal Ataturk*. The change was made to help modernize the economy and culture of Turkey. Other Altaic languages are spoken in an 8,000-km-wide band of Asia between Turkey and Mongolia and China, including *Azerbaijani*, *Bashkir*, *Chuvash*, *Kazakh*, *Kyrgyz*, *Mongolian*, *Tartar*, *Turkmen*, *Uighur*, and *Uzbek*. The Soviet Union suppressed the use of these languages, and forced the use of the ***Russian Cyrillic Alphabet*** on a population familiar with Arabic letters. With the fall of the Soviet Union, many of these languages have been recognized by the newly independent countries of *Azerbaijan*, *Kazakhstan*, *Kyrgyzstan*, *Turkmenistan*, and *Uzbekistan*. New countries don't always follow cultural boundaries, dividing speakers of such Altaic languages as *Bashkir*, *Chuvash*, *Tatar,* and *Uighur*.

Uralic Languages (173): Proto-Uralic was first used 7,000 years ago by people living in the Ural Mountains, north of the Kurgan homeland. Migrants took the language to *Estonia*, *Finland* and *Siberia*. A second branch took the language to *Hungary*.

African Language Families (173): Africa has nearly 1,000 documented languages and several thousand named dialects. People lived in relative isolation for at least 5,000 years. Only ten are spoken by more than 10 million people. Few have a written tradition aside from the documentation done by missionaries in using either Latin or Arabic alphabets.

Principal Language Families in Sub-Saharan Africa (173): In northern Africa, Afro-Asiatic *Arabic* dominates language use in a multitude of dialects. Other Afro-Asiatic languages spoken by more than 5 million Africans include *Amharic*, *Oromo*, and *Somali* in the Horn of Africa and *Hausa* in northern Nigeria.

Niger-Congo Language Family (173): The ***Niger-Congo family*** has six branches that include more than 95% of Sub-Saharan African speakers. The remaining 5% speak languages in the ***Koisan*** or ***Nilo-Saharan*** families. Several million speakers employ either *English* or *Afrikaans*, a language which has evolved from Dutch colonial time. The largest branch is *Benue-Congo*, dominated by *Swahili*, the official language only of Tanzania. It is the *lingua franca* for much of eastern Africa. It is a mixture derived from

African groups coming in contact with Arab traders. It is unique in its strong literary tradition.

Nilo-Saharan and Khoisan Language Families (173-174): These families are spoken in north central Africa. There are fewer speakers and six branches: *Fur, Koma, Maba, Saharan, Songhai,* and *Chari-Nile,* further broken up into four groups *Berta, Kunama, East Sudanic,* and *Central Sudanic*–divided into ten subgroups. The *Khoisan* family is in the southwest; they employ clicking sounds.

Austronesian Language Family (174): Austronesian languages are spoken on islands in the *South Pacific.* The people of *Madagascar* speak *Malagasy* even though they are separated by 3,000 km from any Austronesian language speaking people. It is believed people sailed in small boats to Madagascar approximately 2,000 years ago.

Nigeria: Conflict Among Speakers of Different Languages (174-175): Nigeria has had continuous problems dealing with the presence of many languages. More than 200 distinct languages are used, none by a majority of the population. English, the official language, is spoken by 2% of the population, residual from colonial times. *Hausa* is spoken in the north by approximately 25% of the total population. *Ibo* is spoken in the southeast as well as *Efik* and *Ijaw.* In the southwest, *Yoruba* and *Edo* are of importance.

Language Complexity: A Matter of Scale (175): Three-fourths of the world's population speak languages from the Indo-European and Sino-Tibetan families. Nevertheless, there is amazing diversity of language usage around the world. Diversity among people also comes from cultural differences. Speakers of the same language are often very different. Language is only one part of culture.

Development Of Dialects In English (176): ***British Received Pronunciation*** (BRP) is recognized around the world as standard British speech. It is the form used by the media.

Dialects in England (176-178): ***Dialects*** reflect the relationship between culture and the landscape. They develop distinctive distribution through various social processes, such as ***migration, interaction,*** and ***isolation.*** A dialect reflects unique characteristics of the physical environment in which a group lives, and languages change partially in response to modifications of the landscape. Old English developed many regional dialects depending on settlers: *Kentish* in the southeast, *West Saxon* in the southwest, *Mercian* in the center of the island, and *Northumbrian* in the north. When English reemerged after the French invasion, five major regional dialects had emerged: *Northern, East Midland, West Midland, Southwestern,* and *Southeastern* or *Kentish.* The French influenced the way everyone spoke, though the dialects' regions remained essentially the same. The dialect from London, Cambridge, and Oxford emerged as the standard through the use of the printing press–grammar and spelling books were written based on the London dialect. As was the case with language families and individual languages, the dominance of one dialect over others within a country is a measure of the relative political strength of the speakers of the various dialects. Distinct regional dialects still exist though they can be grouped into three main ones: Northern, Midland, and Southern.

English in North America (178-179): The English spoken in modern America owes most of its attributes to the earliest colonists. Other language speakers were acculturated and spoke English while contributing significantly to the language.

Differences Between British and American English (179-180): Isolation provided the means for independent growth of the two which now differ in *vocabulary, spelling,* and *pronunciation*. New objects, features and places were often given Native American names. New inventions have been named differently in the two places. Spelling differs due to **Noah Webster**, the author of the first Webster's American Dictionary. He wrote grammar and spelling books unique to the Americas, hoping to develop a national language to increase internal unity while reducing ties to England. Pronunciation differs for many reasons, including isolation, differences in class backgrounds, and the fact that speech patterns changed more in England than America.

Dialects in the United States (180-183): The original thirteen colonies along the Atlantic Coast can be organized into three areas: New England, Middle Atlantic, and Southeastern. New England was composed mainly of Puritans from southeastern England and a few from northern England. The Middle Atlantic was settled by a diverse group including Quakers from north England, Scots, Irish, Germans, Dutch, and Swedes. The Southeastern area was settled by people from the southeast of England with a multitude of socioeconomic backgrounds. Individual dialects still exist in the eastern U.S., though distinctions diminish with increased communication and transportation. An *isogloss*, the boundaries for the geographic extent of word usage for words not used nationally, helps in the study of dialects. Isoglosses are more difficult to draw for pronunciations than for word usage. Pronunciation is much more easily recognized, as with the strong southern and New England accents. Mobility has created a more uniform language in the west.

African-American Dialects of English (183): The ***African-American dialect*** has roots in the forced migration of African natives for the slave trade. A distinct dialect was preserved so that they could speak without being understood by their white masters. Many African-Americans migrated to the cities of the north, retaining their dialect. Today, the dialect is preserved, playing a central role as an identifying factor of a distinct culture.

Global Dominance of English (183): English has become the ***lingua franca*** for much of the world. It is used in communication, business, schools, research, and medicine; it is seen in pop culture; and it is necessary for smaller countries that want to participate more fully in world affairs.

CLOSING REMARKS

Language is integral to human beings. Communication exists because people have found, through time, common representations for thoughts, expressions, objects, and actions. Language can be as widespread as English or as isolated as Basque but its importance does not change. People move, taking culture (and language) with them where it either remains relatively intact or changes reflecting new influences from other people, environments, or experiences. The reader of the present Study Guide can participate in this learning experience owing to a common language–English.

Family → Branch → Grp

KEY TERMS AND CONCEPTS

Language: A system of communication through speech, a collection of sounds that a group of people understands to have the same or similar meaning. Language may be written, verbal, or visual.

Literary Tradition: A written version of a language. A language may or may not have a written form.

Verbal Language: A language which is spoken and heard; speech. Many languages only exist in a verbal form with history passed down in stories which must be remembered.

Language Family: Includes individual languages related through a common ancestor that existed before recorded history. There are six main language families, with numerous other languages in either very small families or which are independently classifiable.

Language Branch: Includes languages that share a common origin, but have further evolved into individual languages.

Language Group: Comprises individual languages within a branch that share a common origin in the relatively recent past, and display relatively few differences in grammar and vocabulary.

Dialect: Form of a language spoken in a local area. There can be countless dialects which are all part of a given language.

Standard Language: The dialect of a language which is used for government, business, education, and mass communication.

Place of Origin: The place or area from which a given language family, branch, group, or dialect stems. American English can trace its origins back to England.

Diffusion: The spreading of a concept across the landscape, usually accompanied by the movement of people.

Official Language: A language adopted for use by a government.

Lingua franca: A language used in commerce by people who have different native languages. English is rapidly becoming the lingua franca for handling world matters such as business, communication, government activities, and international media.

Pidgin Language: A language constructed by learning a few of the grammar rules and words of a lingua franca while mixing in some elements of their own languages.

Germanic Languages: The Germanic branch of the Indo-European family includes West, North, and East Germanic groups. The original Germanic language has been lost though speakers lived at least across central and northern Europe.

West Germanic Group: Comprised of High and Low Germanic languages from the south and north of present day Germany. High Germanic has evolved into modern German, while Low Germanic has evolved into English (an official language of the United Nations) and the Low German dialects–Dutch, Flemish, and Frisian.

North Germanic Group: Old Norse is the language which has evolved into the Scandinavian languages of Swedish, Danish, Norwegian, and Icelandic.

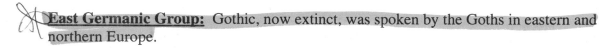**East Germanic Group:** Gothic, now extinct, was spoken by the Goths in eastern and northern Europe.

Extinct Language: A language which is no longer spoken or read in daily activities by anyone in the world. Gothic and Latin are both extinct languages. Some have been revived, such as Cornish from Cornwall, England.

Indo-European Language Family: A language family with nearly three billion speakers; important artistic and literary traditions; and eight branches, including Germanic, Romance, Balto-Slavic, Indo-Iranian, Albanian, Armenian, Greek, and Celtic.

Romance Language Branch: Evolved from the dispersal of Roman soldiers during the reign of the Roman Empire. Contains two of the official languages of the United Nations, Spanish and French, as well as Portuguese, Italian, and Romanian of Romania and Moldova, as well as other less prolific languages. This branch is most familiar to English speakers.

Vulgar Latin: The form of Latin spoken by "the masses" of the populace as well as being the version spoken by Roman soldiers, which was then transmitted to the provinces. The dialects that arose through time differences and different regional languages have evolved even further to become separate and distinct languages.

Standard National Language: A language adopted by a government or governments in order to facilitate communication. A standard language tends to change all dialects in favor of the dominant dialect.

Creolized Language: A language resulting from the mixing of a colonizer's language with the indigenous language of the people being dominated.

Indo-Iranian Language Branch: The most prolific of the Indo-European language branches with more than 100 individual languages, more than one billion people, and two main groups–Indic and Iranian.

Indic Language Group: Second largest language group in world, encompassing language of India, Pakistan and Bangladesh. Hindi and Urdu are the most important languages, though there are many others.

Devanagari: The script used since the seventh century to write the multitude of Hindi dialects. Few people write the language, which has kept it from evolving as has the verbal language.

Arabic Alphabet: The script generally used by Muslims or in countries which have come in contact with Islam. The script used to write the Quran, the holy book of Islam.

Hindustani: The original language of Urdu and Hindi.

Iranian Language Group: Includes languages spoken in Iran and neighboring countries in southwestern Asia. All are written with the Arabic alphabet

Balto-Slavic Language Branch: Originally Slavic, the group contains closely related languages of Asia and central Europe.

East Slavic Group: Contains Russian, one of the official languages of the United Nations. The lingua franca for the countries of the former Soviet Union.

Baltic Group: Latvian and Lithuanian are the principle languages of this group, spoken primarily around the Baltic Sea.

West Slavic Group: Polish is the most widely spoken language, followed by Czech and Slovak. Differences in the latter two have been cause for a great deal of unrest in former Czechoslovakia.

South Slavic: Examples include Bulgarian as well as Serbo-Croatian, essentially the same language with different literary traditions being written with the Cyrillic and Roman alphabets, respectively.

Cyrillic Alphabet: An alphabet using some of the characters from the Grecian's ancient form of writing. It is a phonetic alphabet, each symbol representing a spoken sound.

Roman Alphabet: The alphabet used by the ancient Romans to write Latin. It has evolved into the script now being read. It is a phonetic alphabet as well.

Celtic Branch: The languages of most of Europe, northern Europe and the British Isles from about 2000 years ago. It now exists in two groups, Goidelic and Brythonic which have become Irish Gaelic, Scottish Gaelic, and Breton.

Proto-Indo-European Language: The precursor to the Indo-European Language family, with at least two theories for location of the hearth.

Basque: An anomalous survivor from before Indo-European languages. It is believed to be completely unrelated to Indo-European languages.

Isolated Languages: Languages which are unrelated to any other language and are, therefore, not attached to any language family.

Sino-Tibetan Language Family: The People's Republic of China and smaller countries in southeast Asia have languages in this family. There are three branches: Sinitic, Austro-Thai and Tibetan-Burman.

Sinitic Branch: The main languages of China fall into this branch. Mandarin is spoken by 75% of the population and is an official language of the UN, China, and Taiwan. The languages are composed of 420 one-syllable words, and meaning is inferred from context in sentences and the tone of voice of the speaker.

Ideograms: Written symbols which represent ideas or concepts rather than pronunciation.

Austro-Thai Branch: Mainly the Thai language of Laos, Thailand, and parts of Vietnam.

Tibeto-Burman Branch: The principal language is Burmese used in Myanmar.

Japanese Language Family: The island location of Japan has allowed the language to evolve into a language structurally different from those of China, despite the introduction of cultural traits. It is written using both ideograms and phonetic symbols.

Korean Language Family: Separate language family, though related to both Japanese and the Altaic languages. More than half the vocabulary is Chinese.

Hankul: The writing system for Korean; each letter represents a sound.

Diacritical Marks: Marks placed above letters to show different pronunciations in a written language.

Austro-Asiatic Language Family: This family includes Arabic, Hebrew, Aramaic, and others. It is the language family used for the holy books of three major world religions–the Judeo-Christian Bible and the Islamic Quran.

Arabic: The dominant language of the Austro-Asiatic language family with over 200 million native speakers. It is an official language of the United Nations. It is relatively standardized due to the Quran.

Hebrew: It is a modern language revived in the twentieth century after it died out in the fourth century. It is the official language of Israel, reinstated to bring unity to the varied Jewish population.

Eliezer Ben-Yehuda: The father of modern Hebrew. He wrote modern grammar rules, invented many words, and wrote the first modern Hebrew dictionary.

Altaic Language Family: Is used in a band 8,000 km long in Asia between Turkey and Mongolia and China. Turkish is the main language though there are several others in this area as well.

Uralic Language Family: An ancient language with relatively known origins; it is now spoken in Estonia, Finland, Siberia, and Hungary.

African Language Families: There are nearly 1,000 different African languages and thousands of dialects. Only ten are spoken by more than 5 million people, due to isolation of people from one another.

Niger-Congo Language Family: Has six branches which encompass more than 95% of Sub-Saharan speakers.

Swahili: The strongest language of eastern Africa. Used as the lingua franca for the diverse peoples of this area.

British Received Pronunciation (BRP): The dialect of English associated with the upper-class Britons living in the London area, and now considered standard in the United Kingdom.

Noah Webster: Promoted the use of American English to unify the people of the Americas as separate from England.

Isogloss: A boundary separating regions in which different language usage predominates.

1. The written version of a language is called a _____ tradition.   literary

2. Language relatedness can be broken down into a hierarchy of families, _____, _____, _____, and dialects.   branches, groups, languages

3. The _____-_____ language family contains 50% of the speakers of the world.   Indo-European

4. The second most important language family is the _____-_____, with 20% of the world's population.   Sino-Tibetan

5. Another 20% speak languages in the Austronesian, _____-_____, _____-_____, and Dravidian language families.   Afro-Asiatic, Niger-Congo

6. Language diffuses through _____.   migration

7. English has become the world's main _____ _____, used in business, commerce, government and other world matters.   lingua franca

8. The six official language of the United Nations are Spanish, _____, _____, _____, Mandarin Chinese, and Arabic,   French, English, Russian

9. England was invaded in 450 A.D. by the _____, _____, and _____ which provided the basis for modern English.   Angles, Jutes, Saxons

10. English is a _____ _____ (group) language.   Low Germanic

11. The first known occupants of the British Isles from around 2000 B.C. were the _____.   Celts

12. Swedish, Danish, Norwegian, and Icelandic are all North Germanic languages, stemming from Old _____, a common ancestor   Norse

13. Of the Scandinavian languages, isolation stunted the growth of _____, making it an interesting language to study.   Icelandic

14. _____, an East Germanic group language, is now an _____ _____ meaning it is no longer used or spoken in day to day life by anyone.   Gothic, extinct language

15. The Indo-European language family consists of eight language branches, the four most significant have a total of 1.6 billion speakers: _____, _____, _____-_____, and Indo-Iranian as well as the Albanian,   Germanic, Romance, Balto-Slavic

Armenian, Greek and Celtic branches

16. The Romance language branch stems from the _____ spoken by the ancient Romans.   Latin

17. In an effort to unify the Roman Empire, other languages were _____ or _____ in favor of Latin.   suppressed, extinguished

18. _____ _____ is the common form of the language spoken by the Roman soldiers who occupied the provinces.   Vulgar Latin

19. In the fifth century the _____ of the _____ Empire cut off communication between the various provinces, which left them isolated from one another.   collapse, Roman

20. Romance languages are the group most familiar to English speakers, the four most widely used modern languages being _____, _____, _____, and _____.   Spanish, Portuguese, French, Italian

21. Isolation across Europe is due mostly to intervening obstacles, _____ _____, which make communication and travel difficult.   natural boundaries

22. _____ is the second language of Spain.   Catalan

23. Speakers of Portuguese are attempting to _____ the language to enable communication and the exchange of such things as movies, television programs, music and literature   standardize

24. A _____ _____ can be constructed using a lingua franca as a base and adding elements of the native language.   pidgin language

25. A _____ _____ is a mixing of an indigenous language with that of a conquering people.   creole language

26. The _____-_____ language branch is the largest of the Indo-European family and its _____ group is the second largest language group in the world   Indo-Iranian, Indic

27. _____ is a collection of languages from India.   Hindi

28. There are numerous written scripts including, though certainly not limited to _____, _____, _____, _____, ideograms, hankel, and phonetic alphabet.   Latin, Arabic, Devanagari, Cyrillic

29. India has _____ established official languages recognized by the   fourteen

government.

30. The _____-_____ language branch has relatively few differences between languages, and has a common ancestor of _____.

Balto-Slavic

Slavic

31. The most widely used language of this branch is _____, one of the six official languages of the UN. It has become the lingua franca for the republics formed in the post Communist era.

Russian

32. The West Slavic Group is dominated by speakers of _____, followed by the _____ and _____ who, while united in one country, tried to balance the use of the two languages. They are now separated into the two countries of the _____ _____ and _____.

Polish,
Czech, Slovak
Czech Republic,
Slovakia

33. The South Slavic languages include Serbo-Croatian and Bulgarian, the former being a language spoken by Serbs and Croats, the difference being their written language, using the _____ and _____ alphabets.

Cyrillic, Roman

34. There are two proposed _____, or places of origin, for the Indo-European languages: _____ and _____.

hearths,
Kurgan, Anatolia

35. There are many languages unrelated to any other nor attached to a language family, such as Basque a pre-Indo-European language, which are called _____ languages.

isolated

36. _____ is the Chinese language spoken by 75% of its population and adopted as an official language of the United Nations.

Mandarin

37. Their 4,000 year old written language uses thousands of _____ most of which are _____, representing ideas or concepts.

characters, ideograms

38. _____ and _____ are two language families which have developed in relative geographic isolation from other cultures.

Japanese, Korean

39. Afro-Asiatic languages were used to write the holy books of three major world religions: _____, _____, and _____.

Judaism, Christianity,
Islam

40. _____ is the dominant language of the Afro-Asiatic language family with 200 million native speakers and the Quran (which serves as the language standard), and is an official language of the United Nations.

Arabic

41. Hebrew is a revived _____ language, essentially recreated by _____ _____-_____ to unify the populace of Israel.

extinct, Eliezer Ben-
Yehuda

42. Africa is populated by nearly _____ distinct languages and several thousand dialects. Language history of Africa is difficult to trace due to a lack of much _____ _____.

1,000, written tradition

43. Nigeria is plagued by problems which arise from a great deal of cultural diversity seen in the _____ distinct languages used, the most wide spread of which is _____.

200,
Hausa

44. _____ is an anomalous African language with an extensive body of literature.

Swahili

45. _____ _____, the father of American English, started the now long upheld tradition of the Webster's American Dictionary.

Noah Webster

branch → denomination → sect

CHAPTER FIVE

RELIGION

OVERVIEW

Religions were born in a hearth, they diffused across the landscapes of the world, and they have unique distributions. Geography helps us understand the spread of religions around the Earth, as well as the changes they bring to human culture, architecture, and the physical environment. Sometimes religions compete for constituents, and the resulting clashes have often lead to conflict, as in the conflicts continually occurring in the Middle East. Chapter Five investigates many aspects of religion, and how different places have come to accept religion.

SELECTED NOTES

Religion Traits (195): Religions that attempt to appeal to people all over the world are *universalizing religions*. However, some religions may be based on the physical characteristics of a place; these are dubbed *ethnic religions*. Ethnic religions may be more provincial in scope due to their limited appeal. The three main universalizing religions, *Christianity, Islam,* and *Buddhism*, believe in one all-powerful God. They are *monotheist*. On the other hand *polytheist* religions believe there are different Gods serving different functions in the universe. Religions can be generally divided into three levels, the largest of which is a *branch*, the fundamental division. Then it breaks down into a *denomination*, the next lowest level. Finally, the *sect* is a relatively small denominational group which has broken away from the established church.

Christianity (195-199): The largest religion in the world, by far, is Christianity; its nearly *two billion followers* make up about one-third of the world's population. It is the primary religion in North America, South America, Australia, and Europe. It also has a presence in Africa and Asia. Christianity is based upon the teachings of *Jesus*, a Jew born in Bethlehem who preached the gospel of God. Due to the faith his followers had in him he was given the name *Christ*, the Greek word for *messiah* which means *anointed*. Christianity's hearth is in *Palestine*, and it has spread through relocation diffusion and contagious diffusion. *Missionaries* helped spread the influence of Christianity through relocation diffusion. A famous missionary in Christianity, *Paul*, took Christianity to many parts of the Roman Empire. Believers who had daily contact with pagan non-believers also spread Christianity. *Pagan* is a word that was once used to describe a follower of a polytheistic religion. Christianity has three primary branches: Roman Catholic, Eastern Orthodox, and Protestant. Each branch has unique rituals that often deviate from the other branches. *Roman Catholics* believe in the teachings in the Bible as they are interpreted by the church hierarchy, headed in Rome by the Pope. *The Eastern Orthodox* church split with Rome in 1054, and rejects doctrines from Rome added since the eighth century. Eastern Orthodox and Roman Catholics believe in the *seven sacraments* which are rituals that strengthen an individual's ties with God. *Protestantism* was begun by Martin Luther, a German, in 1517 when he posted his ninety-five theses on a church door; they said a person should communicate directly to God, rather than perform sacraments.

Distribution of Christianity (199-202): The distribution of the branches of Christianity in Europe can be observed in Figure 5-4. Roman Catholics dominate in the southeast and southwest, while Protestants are strong in the northwest, and Eastern Orthodox are common in the east and southeast of Europe. Northern Ireland is an example where conflicting religious values lead to hostilities between groups. *Ireland* was a British colony until, in 1937, it was granted independence. It became a republic in 1949. However, the people in its six northern colonies, being mostly Protestant like Great Britain, voted to remain in the United Kingdom. The minority status of the Catholics made them into second-class citizens who are excluded from the best jobs and schools in the six counties. The *Irish Republican Army (IRA)* worked to bring unity to Ireland by means of force. A Protestant equivalent, the *Ulster Defense Force (UDF),* worked to retain the ties with Grat Britain by the same means of force, except they targeted Catholics instead of Protestants. In the Western Hemisphere, Roman Catholics dominate Latin America and the Canadian province of Quebec. Protestants are the majority in the remaining parts of the U.S. and Canada, though pockets of strong Catholic influence remain. Among Protestants in the U.S., Baptists dominate the old South of the U.S., while Methodists and Lutherans tend to dominate in more northerly states. The dominant religions of areas within the U.S. can frequently be traced to the European homelands of the migrants who settled those areas. The *Mormon Church*, founded by Joseph Smith in the early 1800's, is concentrated in the areas near Salt Lake City, Utah. There are a few, relatively small Christian churches that have survived in Egypt, Armenia, Lebanon, Azerbaijan, and Ethiopia.

Islam (203-205): North Africa to Central Asia is dominated by Islam. Islam was founded by its Prophet, *Muhammad,* who was born in *Makkah.* The Angel Gabriel gave Muhammad the elements of the gospel (and he, in turn, put them into the holy book of Islam, the *Quran*). The word Islam means *submission to the will of God*, who is known as *Allah* to Muslims. A Muslim is a practitioner of Islam. Muslims believe in one God, as do Christians, and they believe in the *five pillars*, which are the fundamental manifestations which a Muslim should fulfill in order to remain devout. After being unsuccessful in preaching his gospel in his home city of *Makkah*, Muhammad migrated to *Madina,* where people listened to and adopted his declarations. By Muhammad's death in 632, he had converted most of present day Saudi Arabia to Islam. Muslims trace their religion, along with Jews and Christians, to the children of Abraham. Jews and Christians follow Sarah and her son Isaac; Muslims trace Abraham's second wife Hagar and their son, Ishmael, as their ancestors. Ishmael is thought to be an ancestor of the prophet, Muhammad. After Muhammad's death, his successors spread the influence of Islam from

France to southeastern Europe and northern Africa to Central Asia and on to Indonesia. For seven-hundred years Islam occupied the Iberian Peninsula and, for less time, parts of France; it was expelled in 1492 from Western Europe. Since Islam is a universalizing religion, it is more easily grasped by people of different cultures. *Sunni* and *Shiite* are Islam's two main branches. Sunnis are the largest branch; eighty-three percent of all Muslims belong to it. The main conflict between these two groups is over the line of succession from Muhammad, which determines the divine interpreter of the Quran. The Shiites dominate Iraq and Iran. The Shah of Iran and the Ayatollah Khomeni competed for the leadership of the Shiite branch until the Ayatollah won, due to his stricter adherence to the Islamic statutes.

Nation of Islam (205): In 1930, *Elijah Muhammad* founded the *Nation of Islam* in Detroit. Black Muslims lived austerely and wanted an autonomous nation within the U.S.. *Malcolm X* broke off from Nation of Islam in 1963, after he made a pilgrimage to Makkah to join the orthodox Muslim religion. Two years later he was assassinated; many people suspect the Nation of Islam of murdering Malcolm X. After Elijah Muhammad's death in 1975, his son Wallace took the movement closer to the orthodox church. However, splinter groups adopted the original name of Nation of Islam and continues to follow the separatist teachings of Elijah Muhammad..

Buddhism (205-207): Over 300 million people follow the universal religion of Buddhism, mainly in China and Southeast Asia. Buddhists follow the Four Noble Truths as their guidance to clean living. *Siddhartha Gautauma* founded Buddhism in 563 B.C. in what is modern day Nepal, near India. Although he was privileged due to his status as the son of a lord, he one day realized that he could no longer enjoy his amenities because other people were suffering. After spending six years in a forest, Siddhartha emerged as the *Buddha*, or the *"enlightened one."* Buddhism did not expand much beyond its hearth for three-hundred years. At this time a converted emperor named Asoka attempted to establish the social principles of Buddhism into his empire. Descendants of Asoka sent missionaries to outside territories and gained strong footholds in China, Southeast Asia, and Japan. Ironically, during the same period, Buddhism lost much of its support in India. Like Christianity and Islam, Buddhism has more than one branch. *Theravada* Buddhists believe that, in order to be a good Buddhist, one must become a monk and study full time in order to become enlightened. *Mahayana* is a less-strict form of Buddhism which emphasizes helping others and teaching others, rather than self-introspection. Many Buddhists (especially in China and Japan) believe simultaneously in other religions.

Hinduism (208): The largest ethnic religion in the world is *Hinduism* with *700 million* followers. Hinduism is a pre-historic religion; the earliest documents relating to it date back to 1500 B.C.. Hinduism was brought to India in 1400 B.C. by invading Aryan tribes from Central Asia. The Aryans first settled the Punjab area of northern India. Intermingling for centuries with the native Dravidian populations did modify the religious beliefs of the Aryans. Hinduism allows people to worship its gods in very personal, unique ways; there is no rule book that dictates a universal technique. Furthermore, Hinduism divides the entire population into four primary castes, each of which are broken down into thousands of sub-castes. The *caste system* is a hierarchical division of society in which some castes have social dominance over others. The lowest caste known as the *untouchables* had limited legal rights in India until recent years.

Ethnic Asian Religions (208-209): The teaching and philosophy of Confucius has became a religion in China. *Confucianism* is described as ethical principles for leading a good, orderly life. *Taoism*, originates from the writings of *Lao-Zi,* a contemporary of Confucius. His writings emphasized the mystical and magical aspects of life, rather than public service emphasized by the writings of Confucius. Today, Taoism is practiced in China and Taiwan. Since ancient times the distinct ethnic religion of Japan has been *Shintoism*. Shintoists consider forces of nature such as rocks, rivers, mountains, and trees to be divine. The Japanese Emperor Meiji decided that the emperor was divine also, making Shintoism both a political and religious institution. Many people in Japan believe both in Buddhism and Shintoism.

Ethnic Mediterranean Religions (210): *Judaism* is an ethnic religion based in the eastern Mediterranean Sea. Abraham is considered the father of Judaism. The roots of Christianity and Islam are found in Judaism; Jesus and Abraham were both Jews. In A.D. 70 the Romans dispersed the Jews from Palestine, thus spreading Jews around the world, mainly to Europe. Historically, Jews were forced to live in ghettos in the less desirable parts of European cities. However, during the 1930's and early 1940's European Jewry was mostly killed off and forced to emigrate abroad, with many immigrating to the U.S.. Today, six million of the eighteen million Jews worldwide live in the U.S.. Four million live in Israel.

Ethnic African Religions (210-211): Many African people believe that inanimate objects such as rocks and plants as well as thunderstorms and earthquakes are animated and have spirits. Such beliefs are called *animist*. Many animist beliefs are ultimately related to monotheist system. The events and objects that are animist are below God, in a hierarchical sense. Missionaries from Christianity and Islam have converted many Africans. Christianity is now the most popular single religion in Africa.

Zoroastrianism (211): For a thousand years *Zoroastrianism* was the ethnic religion of the Persian Empire (present day Iran). *Zoroaster* was its founder; he believed that a person was responsible for his own destiny and was ultimately judged by the good or bad deeds performed while on Earth. After Islamic invaders conquered Persia in the seventh century A.D., it completely disappeared from Persia. However, a substantial colony of Zoroastrians remains in Bombay, India.

Cosmogony (211-212): A set of beliefs concerning the origin of the universe is *cosmogony*. Daoism and Confucianism believe that all things are made up of two dynamic, opposing forces: *Yin* and *Yang*. The principles of yin and yang are responsible for all events, and are ever-changing. Christianity and Islam, however, believe that God created the universe for humans to inhabit. Christians view their presence as more of a partnership with God, whereas Muslims believe God bears the responsibility for the

Earth's creation. Some people believe that natural disasters such as floods are the actions of God, yet Christians believe their efforts can help to minimize the effects of such tragic events. Animists do not attempt to transform the environment to such an extent.

Calendars in Religion (212-214): Many ethnic religions around the world have calendars that are based in conjunction with agricultural events. For example, Judaism's holiest days, **Rosh Hashanah** and **Yom Kippur**, occur in the Fall when people traditionally have prayed for enough rain to nourish and sustain their crops. Passover is the time when Jews have offered God the first fruits of the Spring harvest. Shavot (Feast of Weeks) is at the end of the grain harvest. The **Bontok** people of the Philippines celebrate similar points in their agricultural cycle and call them **obaya**. In universalizing religions, such as Christianity and Buddhism, the physical landscape is less important for marking holidays than are the significant events of each religion. For example, the birthday of Jesus, Christmas, and the day Jesus died, Good Friday, are very important days in the Christian Calendar. Similarly, the birthday and day of death for Buddha are celebrated widely by Buddhists around the world. In the Christian world we use the solar calendar for our daily events. However, the Jews and Muslims of the world adhere to the lunar calendar, in which months are only twenty-nine days long. Consequently, the Jewish lunar calendar must be supplemented with an additional month every few years. Muslims maintain a strict lunar calendar, therefore their holidays fall in different seasons with different generations. The **solstices** (the longest and shortest days of the year) played major roles in pagan religions of history. For example Stonehenge, an astronomical and worshipping place of the Druids, was set up to have geometric alignments with the Summer and Winter solstices.

Sacred Space (214-218): Rituals of particular religions are practiced in holy places, or shrines. According to an Indian geographer, the places most likely to be considered holy in Indian by Hindus are riverbanks and coastlines. Among these, the **Ganges River** is the holiest water way; millions come to purify themselves by bathing in its waters. Mountains are also considered holy if the Hindi god Shiva is thought to have visited there. In Buddhism, places that were important in the life of Buddha are considered holy. Places where he was born, received enlightenment, gave his first sermon, and died are all regarded as holy. The two holiest places in Islam are the cities of **Makkah** and **Madinah**. In Makkah, Muhammad was born; in Madinah he first successfully converted non-believers. A **pilgrimage** is a journey by religious persons to the holy lands of their religion. For example, Christians make pilgrimages to Jerusalem, and Muslims take pilgrimages (hajj's) to Makkah. Hindus take **tirthas** to Hindu holy places. Better transportation with technology have increased the capacity of people to make pilgrimages to their respective holy places.

Religious Administration (218-221): Some communities within religions are highly **autonomous, or self-governed**. Interaction between groups is rather low. However, at the other end are the **hierarchical religions** which are highly-organized. Roman Catholics are a very hierarchical religion. It is headed by the **Pope** who delegates geographic provinces to the authority of **Archbishops**, who in turn oversee **Bishops**. Each Bishop oversees a diocese, which is a group of **parishes**. Each parish is headed by a **Priest**. The layout of the Catholic Church is not unlike that of a national government, although the boundaries may cross many national borders. The Mormons also exercise a very structured self-government with its largest core in Salt Lake City. Its common level of government is the **ward;** wards are administered by the church's **president** and **board** from Salt Lake City. Of the three universal religions, Islam is the one which provides the **most autonomy**. In the Muslim place of worship everyone is suppose to participate equally in their devotion to God. Strong Islamic ties are facilitated by high degrees of communication and migration. Among Protestant churches Baptists are very unstructured, as are various groups of the United Church of Christ. However, the Lutheran, Methodist, and Episcopalian churches have hierarchies, not very much different from the Roman Catholic Church. Judaism and Hinduism are relatively unstructured.

Sacred Structures (221-223): The **church** is the place at which Christians come to worship God. Christian landscapes have a high density of churches because regular, collective worship is very important to their religion. Early churches were modeled after the Roman building for public assembly, the **basilica.** The Eastern Orthodox and Roman Catholic churches tend to be **more elaborate** while Protestant churches, especially in North America, are typically more modest in their architecture. Muslims pray in **mosques**; unlike churches, mosques are not sanctified, but act as a location for communities to come together to pray. **Minarets** are towers which are features of mosques where a **muzzan** summons people to pray. Hindus pray in temples which are dimly lit and possess images of one or more of the deities to whom it is dedicated. **Pagodas** are temples built to enshrine part of Buddha's body or clothing; they are not meant to be used for congregational worship.

Disposing of Bodies (223-225): Christians, Muslims, and Jews normally bury their dead in plots of land used for that end, cemeteries. Some Christians bury their dead with the feet pointed toward Jerusalem, so they may rise toward God at the second coming of Christ. Mandan Indians of the northern plains pointed the feet of their dead toward the Southeast, for they believed their ancestors originated there. In some places like China, where productive farm land is scarce, cemeteries are burdensome to local agricultural output; the government encourages people to cremate. Hindus prefer to burn their dead in cremation ceremonies that use substantial amounts of wood. Zoroastrians would expose their dead to scavenging birds and animals, keeping the corpses from polluting the elements. In Micronesia, some societies dispose of their dead by burying them at sea.

Religious Settlements and Toponyms (225): A utopian settlement is a settlement that is built around a religious or other idealistic way of life. For example, New Harmony, Indiana and Bethlehem, Pennsylvania were set up by people who wanted the perfect religious society. Salt Lake City, which was based on the plans of Zion which Joseph Smith had acquired, and was founded and developed as a utopian city. Most utopian experiments have long since died out or are no longer inhabited by people of the original denomination. Religious **toponyms** are found in many parts of the U.S., especially where the Catholic Church is present; many cities are named after saints. St. Louis (the French version) and San Diego (the Spanish version) are both examples of religious toponyms.

Religion and Social Change (225-227): Frequently people of different religious persuasions fight with each other or with secular (non religion) groups. For example, in Palestine (or Israel, depending upon one's perspective) the forces of Judaism and Islam are continually entrenched in conflict. When the Aryans invaded India, bringing with them their Hindu religion, they also brought a caste system. All people were divided into four castes; in order of most prominence to least, they are: Brahmans (priests and top administrators), the *Kshatriyas* (warriors), the *Vaisyas* (merchants), and the *Shudra* (farm workers). Below all of these were the *untouchables* caste which had few legal rights until recently. Because one was born into a caste there was no accepted way of moving into a better class. Theoretically, the untouchables were the indigenous people of India who were conquered by the Aryans. Hinduism later survived conquests by the Muslims, as well as the Christian British, and is a cultural trait shared by the majority of Indians.

Orthodox Church in Russia (227): In 1721, Czar Peter the Great made the Russian Orthodox Church part of the government. Yet in the 1917 Bolshevik revolution the church suffered from anti-church policies directed by the new government. As communism lingered, the effectiveness of the church to recruit younger participants declined. With the fall of communism in 1989, the church began to have more people participating in its services.

Buddhism in Tibet and Vietnam (227-228): Tibet has long been a stronghold of the Buddhist religion. In 1950, the Chinese took control of Tibet and exiled the *Dalai Lama*, the head of Tibetan Buddhism. Furthermore, the Chinese government destroyed the monasteries and temples of Buddhism which contained related artifacts and scriptures. The monks were taken from the government fiber as it was reconstructed in the form of a secular institution. Buddhism in Vietnam also suffered through warring by the French and later the Americans. Buddhist temples that were not bombed into rubble by bombing missions suffered neglect from the anti-religious themes of the communist government that ruled all of Vietnam, beginning in 1975.

South Asian Religious Wars (228-230): Around 1000 A.D., the Muslim king Mahmud invaded the Punjab area of northern India, bringing Islam into the realm of Hinduism. Subsequent Muslim invasions were successful in penetrating most of India and converting much of its population through intermarriage and immigration. When the area was freed from British colonial control in 1948, there was another struggle between the two groups for control of South Asia. Instead of joint control, two states were created; *Pakistan* for the *Muslims* and *India* for the *Hindus*. The *Sikh* religion, which has elements of both Hinduism and Islam, has fought for more self-government for its 18 million members. The island country of Sri Lanka has also been torn by civil wars between the Tamil minority and the Sinhalese majority which controls the politics and businesses of the island.

War in the Middle East and the Holy Land (230-234): Since Judaism, Christianity, and Islam all have similar roots, they also see the eastern Mediterranean as their Holy Lands. As a result, competition for control of this land has been a constant source of conflict for militant adherents of each of these religions. By the eighth century, Islamic territory encompassed most of the Middle East, North Africa, the Iberian Peninsula, and parts of France. The Jews dominated in Palestine before they were expelled by the Romans in A.D. 70, not to return in large numbers until 1948, when the state of Israel was created. Jerusalem is the third holiest city of Islam because the rock upon which Muhammad is thought to have ascended to heaven is located there in the Dome of the Rock. Christians consider Palestine holy because Jesus spent his life there, spreading the gospel. During the Crusades, Christians captured Jerusalem a few times, but never held it for a prolonged period of time. The Muslims have held Palestine for most of the time between the seventh century and 1917. Great Britain took control over Palestine after it helped to defeat the Ottoman Empire in 1917. Since the inception of the Israeli state in 1948, it has been involved in four official wars; they occurred in 1949, 1956, 1967, and 1973. During its wars with Arab neighbors, Israel acquired territories such as the Golan Heights, the Sinai Peninsula, and the West Bank. It has used these territories as bartering pieces for peace with the same countries. Palestinians populate much of the territory taken by Israel . Demographically, Palestinians reproduce at much higher rates that do Jews, so in the near future there will be relatively higher Islamic populations in some areas of Israel. The continuing conflicts of the Palestinians and Jews will likely be a source of news for years to come.

Iraq Invading Kuwait (234): The ruling Ba'ath party of Iraq decided to conquer the small Persian Gulf country of Kuwait in 1990. They argued Kuwait was a part of Iraq that was cut apart in the early twentieth century. Nonetheless, other countries were outraged and Iraq was expelled from Kuwait in 1991. Iraqis view the Middle East as a homogeneous society that transcends international borders, with the sole exception being Israel. Iraq, along with other Islamic nations, has stated the removal of Israel from the Middle East as one of its objectives.

Middle East Conflict (238-240): Israel is a very small country which occupies only 8,000 square miles of land. Surrounding it are Islamic Arab countries that occupy ten million square miles, though much of it is unoccupied. Historically, there have been many military engagements between the Arabs and Israelis. Given Israel's small size, it is quite vulnerable to attack. To reduce this vulnerability, the occupied territories of the Golan Heights and the West Bank were captured in wars by Israel and used to reduce military incursions by its enemies. Military conflicts in this part of the world are unwavering, in part due to the rise of *fundamentalism*, which is a strict interpretation of a religion that whips up fervor to "defend the faith."

CLOSING REMARKS

Interestingly, the hearths of Judaism, Christianity, and Islam are in the same geographic region of the Middle East. Although all three religions are very much related in their ancient roots, there are today seemingly endless conflicts among all three faiths. It is pertinent to note how the dominions of each religion has evolved, expanded, and contracted throughout history.

KEY TERMS AND CONCEPTS

Universalizing Religions: A religion that attempts to appeal to all people, not just those living in a particular location. Islam, Christianity, and Buddhism are universalizing religions.

Ethnic Religion: A religion with a relatively concentrated spatial distribution whose principles are likely to be based on the physical characteristics of the particular location in which its adherents are concentrated. These religions are harder-pressed to serve global constituents.

Monotheism: The doctrine or belief in only one God. Christianity, Judaism, and Islam all believe in a single, all-powerful God.

Polytheism: The doctrine or belief in more than one God. Hindus, Ancient Greeks, and Romans all believed in more than one God.

Branch: A large and fundamental division within a religion. For example, Protestantism and Roman Catholicism are branches of the Christian faith.

Denomination: A division within a branch of a religion. For example, Baptists and Methodists are denominations of the Protestant branch of Christianity.

Sect: A relatively small denominational group that has broken away from an established church. Sometimes sects are ostracized by more orthodox church members.

Missionary: An individual who helps to diffuse a universalizing religion. The recruitment of new members is important to the growth of many religions.

Pagan: The follower of a polytheistic religion or one who is irreligious.

Caste: The class or distinct hereditary order into which a Hindu is assigned according to religious law. The lowest caste is the untouchables and the highest caste is the Brahmans.

Ghetto: During the Middle Ages, a neighborhood in a city set up by law to be inhabited only by Jews. Now used to denote a section of a city in which members of any minority group dominates (because of social, legal, or economic pressure).

Animism: Belief that objects (such as plants and stones), or natural events (like thunderstorms and earthquakes), have a discrete spirit and conscious life. This was prevalent in many of the tribes of Africa, though less so now than in the past because of the influence of Islamic and Christian missionaries.

Cosmogony: A set of religious beliefs concerning the origin of the universe. Judaism, Islam, and Christianity believe that God created the universe.

Pilgrimage: A journey to a place considered sacred for religious purposes. For example, Muslims travel to Makkah for their pilgrimage.

Autonomous Religion: A religion that does not have a central authority but shares ideas and cooperates informally. There is little administrative structure in these religions.

Hierarchical Religions: A religion in which a central authority exercises a high degree of control. The Pope and organization of the Roman Catholic church seems a clear example.

Diocese: The basic unit of geographic organization in the Roman Catholic church. Each diocese is headed by a bishop.

Pagoda: The tall, many sided towers that are used by Buddhists and Shintoists for containment of religious articles.

Catacombs: Underground passages used to bury dead Christians when Roman statutes prohibited their religion. After Christianity became legal, the dead were buried in yards near churches.

Solstice: The time of year that the sunlight is the shortest (winter solstice) or the longest (summer solstice). It was a very important date for many ancient religions.

Fundamentalism: Literal interpretation and strict adherence to basic principles of a religion, often leading to intolerant policies between religious groups.

1. The cores from which religions expand are known as _____.   hearths

2. Religions that attempt to appeal to all people are called _____ religions.   universalizing

3. A relatively small group which has broken away from a denomination is a _____.   sect

4. Christianity was founded on the teachings of _____.   Jesus

5. It is the duty of _____ to spread the appeal of a religion, and try to gain converts.   missionaries

6. The followers of polytheistic religions are known by monotheists as _____.   pagans

7. Eastern Orthodox is one of three branches of the _____ religion.   Christian

8. The region of Latin America is dominated by the _____ _____ branch of the _____ religion.   Roman Catholic, Christian

9. The militant organization, the Irish Republican Army, targets _____ in Northern Ireland.   Protestants

10. In Northern Ireland, _____ _____ constitute the largest minority of the population.   Roman Catholics

11. The _____ church clusters around the state of Utah.   Mormon

12. The prophet of _____ is Muhammad.   Islam

13. Islam's holiest city is _____, to which all Muslims who are capable are expected to make a _____ at least once.   Makkah pilgrimage

14. A devout Muslim lives by the _____ _____ of Islam.   five pillars

15. _____ and _____ are the two main branches of Islam.   Sunni, Shiite

16. The U.S. splinter group, The Nation of Islam, was formed in 1930 by _____ _____.   Elijah Muhammad

17. The third-largest universalizing religion, _____ was founded in present-day Nepal by Siddhartha _____.

Buddhism
Gautama

18. Today, most Buddhists live in the East Asian countries of _____ and _____.

China, Japan

19. The largest ethnic religion in the world is _____, with over _____ million believers.

Hinduism,
700

20. Nearly all Hindus reside in _____.

India

21. Systematic division of Indians by class is known as the _____ system, in which the _____ represent the lowest level.

caste
untouchables

22. Confucianism originated in _____ in the fifth century B.C..

China

23. The Jewish state of _____ has existed in modern times since _____.

Israel
1948

24. The sequestering of Jews in certain neighborhoods known as _____ occurred in many European cities during the middle ages.

ghetto

25. Today, there are about _____ million Jews living throughout the world.

18

26. _____ virtually disappeared from Persia after Islam was introduced by invaders.

Zoroastrianism

27. The longest and shortest days of the year, known as the summer and winter _____, were considered sacred by ancient pagans.

solstices

28. The _____ river is the most important waterway to Hindus.

Ganges

29. Muslims also call their pilgrimages to Makkah _____.

hajj

30. _____ religions have very structured governing bodies and geographic provinces.

Hierarchical

31. Muslims gather to pray at _____, while Christians worship in _____.

mosques
churches

32. Martin Luther's theses helped to create the _____ branch of the Christian church.

Protestant

33. The Chinese have _____ Buddhism in Tibet since 1950.   suppressed

34. The Muslims attacked Europe and occupied the _____   Iberian
Peninsula for 700 years following the eighth century.

35. The holiest Muslim place in Jerusalem is the _____ of the   Dome,
_____.   Rock

36. In 1990, _____ invaded its neighbor Kuwait, invoking   Iraq
historical claims that it was part of its territory.

CHAPTER SIX

SOCIAL CUSTOMS ON THE LANDSCAPE

OVERVIEW

People interact with the environments in which they live. As meaning makers, humans establish routines. They establish belief systems to give meaning to the unexplainable. Groups of people interact in ways that become characteristic for the group. Meaningful actions are repeated and become customs. The daily routine has meaning, consciously or not. There is a yearly cycle of events and actions which is repeated. The relation between social customs and the cultural landscape is a fascinating study. People change the natural environment and create landscapes, or built environments, to suit their needs and/or preferences. Geographers are interested in people's interactions with their environments. As communication and transportation become faster and more widely spread, there are few areas in the world which remain completely isolated. Distinctive differences arise when a group of people receives all of their stimuli from within the group and from their environment alone. Regional differences are diminishing with modern technology and communication. English replaces indigenous languages. Levi's replace traditional dress, and rock and roll drones from speakers around the world.

SELECTED NOTES

Folk and Popular Customs (247): People, as lovers of routine, form **habits,** or repetitive acts performed by an individual. **Customs** are repetitive acts of a group performed to the extent that it becomes characteristic of the group. A custom is a habit that a group of people has widely adopted. People in a group manifest the feeling of the group as **culture,** the body of customary beliefs, social forms, and material traits of a group of people. Social customs can be divided into two categories. **Folk customs** are traditionally practiced primarily by small, homogeneous groups living in isolated rural areas. **Popular customs** are found in large, heterogeneous societies that share certain habits despite differences in other personal characteristics. The difference can be seen in the amount of interaction taking place between a group of people and other people. A group develops distinctive customs from experiencing local, social, and physical conditions in isolation from other groups. Groups living in proximity may generate a variety of folk customs in a limited geographic area because of limited communication. In contrast, popular customs are dependent on time. They vary across time and change rapidly rather than varying from place to place at a given time, as is the case with folk customs. Popular customs are diffused quickly through media, communication, and rapid transportation networks. Popular customs are gaining importance around the world, diminishing cultural diversity and changing groups' unique identities. Popular customs threaten the environment through a lack of sensitivity to particularly fragile or unique ecosystems.

Origin of Folk and Popular Customs (247-248): Social customs originate at a **hearth**, or place of origin. Folk customs often have anonymous, multiple, simultaneous hearths, sources, dates of conception, and originators. Popular customs are generally a product of economically developed countries with a strong and stable infrastructure. Technology and increased leisure time generate mass production and the means for acquisition. Leisure time increases when jobs shift from predominantly agricultural (necessary for subsistence living) to service and manufacturing (specialized jobs).

Origin of Folk Music (248): **Folk songs** are anonymous and are orally transmitted. Songs are written about the activities in daily life familiar to the majority of people. They tell stories and transmit information about farming, life-cycle events, mysteries, or beliefs. Themes in folk music are recurrent, and can be traced to multiple hearths. Geographer **George Carney** identified four major hearths for country music in the U.S., based on the birthplaces of people in the field: southern Appalachia, central Tennessee and Kentucky, the Ozark and Ouachita uplands of western Arkansas and eastern Oklahoma, and north-central Texas.

Origin of Popular Music (249): **Popular music** contrasts significantly with folk music. It is written with the express purpose of mass-production and sale. Popular music, as it is now known in the U.S., began around 1900 when music hall and vaudeville shows were main sources of popular entertainment. **Tin Pan Alley**, along 28th Street between Fifth Avenue and Broadway, grew from the demand for catchy, memorable tunes which were then turned to profits by the sale of mass produced copies of sheet music. Tin Pan Alley disappeared after World War II, when recorded music replaced sheet music as the primary source of income. Popular music was made available during the war for the soldiers and civilians overseas through broadcasts by the Armed Forces Radio Network. English became the international language for music.

Diffusion of Folk and Popular Customs (249): Folk songs are communicated orally on a much smaller scale, primarily through migration rather than electronic communication. Popular customs are diffused following a process of *hierarchical* diffusion from *hearths* or *nodes of innovation*. Hollywood, CA and New York City are strong nodes of innovation, both for ideas and for communication means.

The Amish: Example of Relocation Diffusion (249-250): The **Amish** began with a Swiss Mennonite Bishop named Jakob Amman. He established a group of followers and became known as the Amish. They migrated from three areas: Bern, Switzerland; Alsace, France; and the Palatinate region of Germany. The European Amish eventually merged with the common culture. In the 1700s, Amish from Bern and the Palatinate settled in Pennsylvania. A second group followed in the early 1800s and settled in Ohio, Illinois, Iowa and Ontario, encouraged to migrate by promises of cheap land. Relying on less advanced technology and traditional customs, they have left their mark across the landscape of the U.S.. Folk customs dictate every son must receive his own farm, so a single farm in Pennsylvania could be sold and the revenue would buy enough land for the entire family in places like southwestern Kentucky.

Sports: Example of Hierarchical Diffusion (250-252): *Soccer* has grown to be the most popular game in the world. It began as a folk custom in England in the eleventh century when the head of a Danish soldier was found which they began to kick. Boys got the idea of inflating a cow bladder. Early games were played by a mob between villages. The winning village was the one who got the ball to the center of the rival village. In the twelfth century *"football"* was confined to a vacant lot and the rules were standardized. King Henry II outlawed the game in the late 1100's, and it was legalized again by King James I in 1603. It became a popular culture with the game's increased skill of the players and the support of clubs in the 1800s. People began to have time to participate in spectator sports. In 1863 the Football Association was formed to organize professional leagues and to formalize the structure of the sport. *Rugby* was a spin-off, formed when a player at Rugby College picked up the ball and ran with it in 1823. Soccer was exported to continental Europe and onward through contact with English players. The British Empire was a vehicle for diffusion, there being Englishmen migrating around the globe. Russia received the game when a factory near Moscow advertised in London for soccer playing workers. They were absorbed into the culture and Moscow's Dynamo team is the country's most famous. Soccer has never reached the same height of popularity in the U.S. as it has other places. A game was played in the U.S. and, instead of adopting soccer rules, Rugby rules were adopted. The game has evolved into a completely new game–American *football*.

Other Sports (252-254): Every country and culture has its favored game. Organized spectator sports are now a part of popular custom. The common element is people's willingness to pay for the privilege of watching a game. The soccer World Cup final match is the single most watched historical event.

Himalayan Art (254-255): Geographers *P. Karan* and *Cotton Mather* investigated a narrow corridor of 2,500 km in the Himalayan Mountains of Bhutan, Nepal and northern India. They contain four religious groups: Tibetan Buddhists, Hindus, Muslims, and Southeast Asian Animists. Limited interaction and spatial proximity included, there are four distinctive folk customs reflected in artwork, based on beliefs about the world around them as well as the actual natural environment.

Distinctive Food Preferences (255): People adapt their food preferences to conditions in the environment. What isn't available can't be eaten. *Soybeans* are widely grown in Asia. They have to be processed as they are toxic in their raw state and indigestible. Fuel is scarce in Asia, so they can't be subjected to a lengthy cooking process. Instead bean sprouts, bean curd, and soy sauce are eaten. Fuel shortages in Italy have created a preference for quick-frying foods. In northern Europe, availability of fuel has developed preferences for slowly stewed and baked foods.

<u>Food Diversity in Transylvania (255-256)</u>: Food preferences can develop differently while living in close proximity. Culturally diverse people occupy Transylvania and their soups show distinct traditions. Preferences for ingredients range from vegetables, pork, sauerkraut, to cherry tree twigs, curdled milk, goose and others. Every cultural group has its own recipe. Cooking traditions are often evidence of cultural heritage long after acculturation has rendered people indistinguishable from those of the majority.

<u>Food Taboos and Attractions (256-257)</u>: A restriction on behavior imposed by social custom is a *taboo*. Food taboos arise from perceived negative agents or forces in the environment. The Ainus in Japan don't eat otter as it is believed to be a forgetful animal and consumption of it might cause one to become forgetful. *Food attractions* are the opposite. Foods are thought to enhance sought after traits such as love-making, fertility, or strength. Some food taboos may have grown out of a concern for the environment. For example, some types of food or animals may only be consumed by a few people, often of high-rank. Americans won't eat insects despite their nutritional value, relied on in developing countries to supplement diet.

<u>Folk Housing (258-259)</u>: French geographer *Jean Brunhes,* a major contributor to human geography's cultural landscape tradition, views the house as being among the essential facts of human geography. *Houses* are the products of both cultural tradition and natural conditions. They are built using available materials, the most common are wood and brick, although stone, grass, sod, and skins are also used. Wood is generally preferred as it is easy to work with. In hot, dry climates, *adobe* bricks are made by baking wet mud in the sun. Stone is used as a primary building material as well as for decoration. Social factors influence choices. People may import preferred materials or find less expensive ways of creating the same effect. House form and orientation may result from customary beliefs or environmental factors. Religious and cultural values are reflected in housing. Sacred walls, arrangement of furniture, sacred corners, number and direction of doors, orientation of the house, sleeping patterns, and subsequent buildings all influence the form a house takes. Many skyscrapers do not number the thirteenth floor. Houses are built to protect humans from the natural environment. In snowy and wet areas, roofs are pitched to facilitate runoff. It may be necessary to avoid the sun or use its energy as much as possible. Areas with similar climates and building materials do not necessarily share ideas about housing. *R. W. McColl's* comparison of four relatively isolated villages in dry, northern and western China yielded four distinct house types, all of which served as protection from the extreme hot and cold temperatures.

<u>U.S. Folk House Forms (259-262)</u>: Houses built across the United States reflect the popular house types of the time and place from which settlers came. Three *hearths* for house types have been identified by *Fred Kniffen,* who considered the house a good reflection of cultural heritage, current fashion, functional needs and the impact of environment: *New England, Middle Atlantic,* and *Lower Chesapeake. New England* is the place of origin for four major types of houses, popular in the 1700s and early 1800s: the *Saltbox, Two Chimney, Cape Cod*, and *Front Gable* and *Wing*. These house types, along with their builders, settled in a band along the northern U.S.. The *Middle Atlantic*

people constructed the *"I"-house* which became the most extensive style in the eastern half of the U.S. and the Midwest. *Lower Chesapeake* houses diffused along the southeast coast. With a quick lesson in architecture, a trained eye can still spot the original patterns of settlement across the United States. Modern regional distinctions are no longer as prominent because rapid communication and transportation systems mobilize ideas and people.

Diffusion of Popular Housing, Clothing, and Food (263-265): Modern technology has influenced the shapes, materials, detailing, and other aspects of housing. Houses built since the 1940s show different trends in building. Fashion is the major influence, rather than cultural heritage, changing housing from a *folk custom* to a *popular custom*. **Modern house styles** were most popular between 1945 and 1960 and included the dominant type, *minimal traditional*, as well as *ranch houses, split-level houses, contemporary* and *shed style houses*. **Ranch** houses are of interest as these single level houses took up a larger lot and encouraged **urban sprawl**. **Neo-Eclectic house styles** have been employed from 1960 to the present. The first style was the *mansard* style, as well as *Neo-Tudor, Neo-French*, and *Neo-colonial* styles. These styles incorporate a large central "great room" into the scheme of things, replacing family and living rooms and making room for the television. Regional differences still exist to some extent in noticeable tendencies. Color, style, floor coverings, garages, porches, and decks all vary regionally.

Rapid Diffusion of Clothing Styles (265-267): Clothing is distributed across the U.S. landscape with little regard for distinctive physical features. Occupation will affect clothing styles a great deal in the more developed countries. Income is a second major influence, with relatively affluent people disregarding and replacing entire wardrobes for the season's latest fashion trends. Mass produced copies of designer clothes are instantly available to the general public. People in more developed countries can travel either in person or from an armchair to see the folk cultures and their dress around the world. Many ideas and items of clothing have come into general usage in more developed countries. *Jeans* acquired an image of youthful independence in the 1960s in the U.S., as young people adopted a style of clothing previously associated with low-status manual laborers and farmers. Jeans have become a world wide phenomenon, fetching unbelievable prices on the black market. Regional preferences for particular styles of jeans have developed, from model to button or zipper fly.

Popular Food Customs (267-268): Consumption of large quantities of alcoholic beverages and fresh produce are characteristic of the food customs of popular societies. In the U.S. consumption of alcohol types tends to be greatest around the area of production. Alcohol consumption is relatively low in areas populated by Mormons and Baptists. Consumption increases with advertising and is relatively high in Nevada, due to gambling and resort activities. Regional variations in produce consumption include Southerners eating okra and other warm-weather crops while folks in California and the Northeast consume large amounts of cooler-weather crops. Consumption of alcohol and produce depend on income and advertising. Other regional variations exist which are inexplicable.

<u>Wine Production (268-270):</u> Grapes can be grown in a variety of locations, though today wine is made primarily in locations where people like to drink it, have a tradition of excellence in making it, and have the money to purchase it. Wines are generally named for the region of production and dated. American wines are named after the grape variety. Monasteries preserved the art of wine making during its decline which paralleled that of the Roman Empire. Wine production has increased in popularity around the world except where religions dominate which prohibit the consumption of alcohol.

<u>Importance of Television (271-274):</u> Television is the most popular leisure activity in relatively developed countries throughout the world. It is also the most important mechanism by which knowledge of popular customs is rapidly diffused around the world. Television ownership skyrocketed after 1945. By the mid 1950s more than 75% of all households in America owned televisions, 85% of the world's 37 million sets. Different levels of television service today fall into four categories: countries where nearly every household has a set (North America, Europe, Australia, New Zealand, and Japan); countries where ownership is common though not universal (wealthier Latin America and poorer European states); countries where televisions exist though not extensively due to cost (Africa, Asia and poorer Latin America); and, finally, about 30 countries (mostly very poor African and Asian) that have relatively few sets. Control of television falls to the private sector's corporations, making a profit by selling advertising time. Private ownership of television companies occurs in America and other Western Hemisphere countries. Most governments control television companies in order to control and censor information distribution. Governments are loosing their tenuous grip on the control of television information. Satellite dishes receive hundreds of channels. Television has been a force for political unrest rather than stability, contrary to *George Orwell's* expectations in his 1949 book <u>1984</u>.

<u>Threat To Folk Customs (274-275):</u> The loss of folk customs is symbolic of the loss of traditional cultural values and cultural dominance by Western perspectives. Folk modes of dress are being replaced by preferences for and the availability of a more developed country's mode of dress. The business suit has become the international dress for businessmen and politicians. Women's roles are also changing. Many cultures have a folk tradition which places women in roles subservient to men. Women have been limited inaccess to education and have been victimized, which limits their advancement. Popular cultures have brought some concepts of legal equality as well as economic and social opportunities outside of the home. Prostitution has increased and is supported in some countries as a major source of income. Lesser developed countries fear the loss of independence through increased infusion of popular customs. The U.S., the United Kingdom and Japan dominate the television industry in most LDC's. Leaders view television as a new method for economic and cultural imperialism. Many characteristically American beliefs conflict with and threaten to drive out traditional social customs.

<u>Western Control of News Media (276):</u> The news gathering capabilities and the network of gathering and distributing the news is more feared than the entertainment function of

televisions. The Associated Press (AP) and Reuters are the dominant world news distributor, American and British owned. The AP and Reuters provide stories for newspapers and radio stations around the world. Visnew Ltd. and Worldwide Television News Corporation (WTN)–British-American owned–supply most of the world's television news video. This external news process is threatening, especially to governments which control the media. It can be argued that news, then, reflects Western values, with biased, unbalanced, and inaccurate views of other countries. During recent times of conflict, the BBC provided the only remotely accurate reporting for local residents during the Persian Gulf War.

Impact of Popular Customs upon the Environment (276-279): Popular customs are going to be less likely to consider the natural environment. They are often imposed on the environment, rather than working within it. Golf has become a very popular leisure time activity and, with its growth, hundreds of golf courses have been developed, recreating the landscape so thatevery hole of the course is perfect. Popular customs can be seen across the U.S.. Promoters of popular customs want a uniform appearance, to generate "product recognition" and greater consumption. There are several chains of restaurants, quick stops, grocery stores, department stores, and motels which recur from coast to coast. Fast-food restaurants are standard. They look alike, smell alike, the food tastes the same and they all have uncomfortable chairs and stools. They are attractive because they are convenient , affordable, and familiar. The landscape around the world is becoming more uniform as popular customs diffuse and stores open. Japanese-style cars dominate consumer preferences around the world. Other auto makers are following the lead by producing cars which are similar in appearance and performance.

Increased Demand for Natural Resources (279-280): Increased consumption requires the increased use of natural resources in production. Natural resources are being consumed, especially petroleum. Animals have become endangered and pushed to extinction. Preference for and means of obtaining increasing amounts of meat have not pushed domestic animals into extinction, rather they are raised in ever larger numbers. With consumption of resources comes pollution of the air, soil, water, and the natural environment in general. Most items produced for popular customs are discarded rather than recycled. Mass production of goods also means a mass production of pollution as solids, liquids, gases, heat, noises, and light.

CLOSING REMARKS

Isolation maintains and encourages diversity. The people of the world come in contact with each other more today than ever in the past. Many own a pair of jeans or have, at the very least, seen them. Tourism is encouraged by LDC's to infuse much needed capital into struggling economies. Contact with people from MDC's is coupled with the spread of popular cultures which, unfortunately, threaten the unique customs of the many diverse peoples of the world.

KEY TERMS AND CONCEPTS

Habit: Repetitive act performed by an individual.

Custom: Repetitive acts of a group performed to the extent that they become characteristic of the group. A custom is a habit that a group of people has widely adopted.

Culture: The body of customary beliefs, social forms, and material traits of a group of people.

Folk customs: Traditionally practiced primarily by small, homogenous groups living in isolated rural areas. They vary more from place to place at a given time.

Popular customs: Found in large, heterogeneous societies that share certain habits despite differences in other personal characteristics. Most Americans wear jeans fairly regularly.

Hearth: Place of origin for a custom, idea, language, or group of people.

Folk Songs: Songs written about daily activities that are anonymous and orally transmitted, often sharing information necessary for life.

George Carney: A geographer who identified four hearths for country music.

Popular Music: Music written specifically for mass distribution and personal gain with a known origin. U.S. Popular Music traditions began in the early 1900's.

Tin Pan Alley: The hearth for early popular music culture, creating massive amounts of sheet music for sale, and for use in vaudeville shows.

Hierarchical Diffusion: Diffusion which occurs from a very strong hearth or node of innovation. U.S. movies are diffused from Hollywood, California.

Amish: A belief system and lifestyle begun in Switzerland in the 1600s by Jakob Amman. The Amish migrated to the Americas in the 1700s and the 1800s. They have had a distinct impact on the landscape.

Soccer: A game diffused from England which has gained immense worldwide popularity and become a popular custom. It is played on a field by two opposing teams which may not touch the ball with their arms nor their hands.

Rugby: Invented in 1823 when a player at Rugby College picked up a soccer ball and ran with it. It has since developed into a separate game and is the precursor for American football.

Football: The name for soccer in other countries. American football is a more physical version of Rugby, developed and popularized by American colleges and universities.

P. Karan & Cotton Mather: Geographers who studied the peoples of a part of the Himalayan Mountains, who found distinct cultural groups which were apparent in their respective forms of artwork.

Soybeans: A crop grown because of its nutritional value. It must be processed and has come to be processed differently depending on availability of fuels.

Taboo: A restriction on behavior imposed by social custom.

Food attractions: Foods consumed because of belief in some inherent trait or substance which will enhance the consumer.

Jean Brunhes: Geographer whose work contributed much to human geography's cultural landscape tradition, studying housing.

House: Structures built to protect people from the natural environment. They are the products of both cultural tradition and natural conditions.

Adobe: A building material made from baking mud in the sun, used in dry, hot areas.

R. W. McColl: Studied four villages in China living in isolation from one another. They developed four distinctly different house types.

Fred Kniffen: Studied the folk house forms of the U.S. and identified three hearths for early house types reflected in subsequent settlement across the country.

Urban Sprawl: A function of people taking up larger and larger areas for houses and properties, rather than using tiny lots and building things very close together.

Jeans: An interesting phenomena in the diffusion of popular culture. They are viewed by some as a symbol for freedom, affluence, America, or the meeting of the masses.

CHAPTER SIX   <u>Progressive Review</u>

1. _____ customs are dependent on time, changing and diffusing very rapidly.   Popular

2. Folk and popular customs derive from the _____ and _____ activities of daily life.   survival, leisure

3. _____ _____ are often anonymous, having multiple hearths and originators while _____ _____ have a known origin and creator.   folk customs, popular customs

4. _____ _____ transmit information orally that is important to a group of people.   Folk songs

5. Popular music began in the early 1900s with _____.   vaudeville

6. The music industry was based in New York at _____ _____ Alley, which was a collection of people in the industry devoted to writing, printing, and selling massive amounts of sheet music.   Tin Pan

7. Popular music started to diffuse during World War II when the Armed Forces _____ _____ transmitted American music overseas.   Radio Network

8. _____ _____ City and _____, _____ are examples of strong nodes of innovation.   New York Hollywood, CA

9. The _____ have made a distinct mark on the American landscape.   Amish

10. Some of the original Amish settlements in _____ are being sold to buy property elsewhere to provide _____ for the _____.   Pennsylvania, farms, sons

11. _____ is the most popular sport in the world.   Soccer

12. _____ and then American _____ were formed from the original soccer game.   Rugby, football

13. People living in _____ tend to develop distinct cultural traits and folk customs.   isolation

14. _____ are a food crop high in protein requiring a great deal of processing to enable digestion.   soybeans

15. Traditions in _____ are evident long after people have been acculturated into a larger group.

cooking

16. Food _____ and _____ are beliefs about food encouraging and discouraging consumption.

taboos, attractions

17. _____ _____ views the house as being among the essential objects for the study of human geography

Jean Brunhes

18. Three hearths for house types in the U.S. are _____ _____, _____ Atlantic, and _____ Chesapeake.

New England, Middle, Lower

19. _____ are a readily recognized item of clothing of popular culture.

Jeans

20. Wines are grown world wide and are named by _____ _____ in the U.S. and by _____ in the rest of the world.

grape variety, region

21. The _____ is the most important tool for spreading information, including popular culture.

television

22. Many folk cultures are being infused by ideas from _____ _____ which have the potential of altering, if not destroying, them.

popular cultures

23. The two main news distributing agencies of the world are owned by people in _____ and _____.

England, U.S.

24. Fast food restaurants, motels and department stores look alike to produce _____ _____.

product recognition

25. Production of goods results in many different types of environmental _____.

pollution

CHAPTER SEVEN

POLITICAL GEOGRAPHY

OVERVIEW

In today's world of the global economy and instantaneous communication people are constantly being given information about places located around the planet. In order to best digest these materials it is imperative to have a good knowledge base of the nations that cover the surface of Earth. Chapter Seven seeks to explain the foundations of Political Geography, which impart an understanding of the cultural and physical factors that determine the events of today's "shrinking" world.

SELECTED NOTES

Changing Borders (288-289): As time passes, so does the configuration of the world's borders. For example, for those who lived in what is now the town of Rittershoffen, France before World War II, their residence would have been within the German border. France annexed part of Germany at the conclusion of the war. Although the European Economic Union has worked to reduce the influence of borders to its members, the function of borders as a barrier has increased in the former Yugoslavia. Today, new borders have been imposed upon the landscape in this area, borders which make trade and travel in these areas more cumbersome than in the past. *Globalization* is the trend which seeks to transfer military, economic, and political authority to a regional authority, while *cultural diversity* is the contrasting idea that desires to give more authority to localized groups of people.

The Definition of a State (289-290): An area organized into a political unit and ruled by an established government is called a *state*. A state has to have *sovereignty*, which is the ability of that country to rule its internal and external affairs without the interference of a second country. In political geography the word *state* is synonymous with *nation* and not with the fifty political subdivisions of the U.S.. Today there are approximately two hundred states. The largest nation on Earth in terms of population is *China* while the largest in terms of area is *Russia*. There are many states with less than one-thousand square kilometers of area; they are mostly islands.

Problems Defining States (290-293): Perceptions vary in the acceptance of some territories as states. After World War II, *Korea* was divided into two states each with a separate and conflicting philosophy on government. Today, although each believes Korea is a nation incomplete without its corresponding half, most of the world acknowledges that two sovereign nations occupy the Korean Peninsula. In 1992, both were admitted to the United Nations as separate countries. *Taiwan* and *China* have a similar relationship. Each claims to have legitimate rule on the entire nation, however the United Nations voted to transfer the ownership of the China seat at the UN to China from Taiwan in 1971. A unique territorial dispute is found in the remote, polar continent of *Antarctica*. Many nations lay claim to this frozen land, but the U.S. and Russia believe no country has authority over this land mass.

The Development of the State (293-296): Before the 1800's much of the Earth's land was unorganized territory. However, early in human history there were a few ancient nations. There were many city-states in the *Fertile Crescent* that stretched from Persia to the Mediterranean. A *city-state* is a sovereign state consisting of a town and the surrounding countryside from which most of its food was derived. Walls clearly marked the area of a city. The ancient state of *Egypt* was situated in the Nile River valley from 3000 B.C. until it was annexed by the Roman Empire in the fourth century B.C.. The *Roman Empire* was the largest ancient nation. It controlled most of Europe, North Africa, and Southwest Asia at its peak. However, it collapsed in the fifth century A.D.. Beginning in 1100 A.D., a few kingdoms had emerged in Europe that would become the modern nations of Great Britain, Spain, and France.

Colonies (296-298): Territory that is legally tied to a sovereign state (rather than being independent) is known as a *colony*. The policy by countries to enlarge their territory through the establishment of colonies is named *colonialism*. European powers sought to establish colonies in other parts of the world in order to spread Christianity, gain wealth, and increase their political influence. The mainland colonies in the Americas rejected foreign rule between 1776 and 1824 in a series of revolutions. Afterward, the European colonial powers led by Britain and France concentrated their efforts on Africa and Asian land. After World War II most of the colonies on these two continents declared their independence. Today, the most populous colony in the world is *Hong Kong*. In 1997 rule over Hong Kong will pass into the hands of the Chinese from the British. The smallest colony in the world is *Pitcairn Island* which is less than two square miles in area and has less than sixty-five people.

What Makes a Nation? (298-301): A *nation* or *nationality* is a collection of people (occupying a particular area of the Earth) who share beliefs such as religion, and cultural characteristics such as language. *Self-determination* is the concept that nationalities have the right to govern themselves without interference. A *nation-state* is a state whose territory corresponds to that particular area. By 1900, most of Europe was comprised of nation-states with the exception of some countries in Eastern Europe. In the 1930's Nazi Germany claimed that all people who spoke their language were essential parts of their country to be re-claimed. Their actions led the world into World War II. *Denmark* is very close to being a true nation-state because it is nearly homogeneously Danish. Even so, there are some ethnic Germans living in Denmark along the border, and some Danes who reside in Germany near the border with Denmark. In order for a state to survive, the populace of the state must share attitudes that support the nation. Such attitudes which unify the populations of nations are known as *centripetal forces*.

Nationalism (301-303): A very strong form of centripetal force is the devotion and loyalty exhibited by the citizens of a state toward said state. This is called *nationalism*. For many states the *mass media* is an effective tool to instill nationalism among their constituents. This can be accomplished in many nations because the newspapers, television stations, and radio stations are often controlled by their governments. Symbols such as flags and patriotic songs also implant nationalistic feelings in many people. When communism fell in Eastern Europe, long suppressed feelings of nationalism erupted from the various ethnic groups, causing many new countries to emerge. In places where the populations of the new countries are varied, as in Bosnia-Hercegovina, many conflicts arise between competing ethnic groups. However, in Slovenia where 90 percent of the residents are Slovenes, the transition from a large country to a smaller country has proceeded without major hostilities.

Shapes of States (303-306): The shape of a state is a part of its identity which is recognized universally. Shapes also contribute to economic and militaristic strategies. There are five basic shapes of states. States where the distance from the center of the country to their perimeter does not vary significantly are *compact states*. These states allow for efficient internal communication. Hungary and Poland are compact states. *Prorupted states* are much like compact states except they have a projecting extension whose function is to interrupt linkages between other countries or to provide access to some resource such as water. *Elongated states* are very long countries which have some parts that are relatively isolated from others. Chile is the best example of the elongated state. Communication is at a disadvantage in this form of state. *Fragmented states* are nations with territory that is not contiguous, such as countries made up of islands. The Philippines and Japan exhibit these traits. Panama is also fragmented by the Canal Zone that bisects it. Fragmented states suffer from poorer communication and poorer integration than other states. A nation which completely surrounds another one is a *perforated state*. South Africa is an example, because it completely engulfs the state of Lesotho. Often the surrounding state has tremendous influence on its internal neighbor.

Landlocked States (306-308): If a country is completely surrounded by one or more countries and has no outlet to the ocean it is considered *landlocked*. Most landlocked countries are found in Africa where fourteen of fifty-four countries are landlocked. This is a geographical legacy from the colonial era when borders were not designed for the advantage the African countries but for the aims of their European occupants. Being landlocked is an economic hindrance because a country has much more difficulty conducting international trade with other countries because it lacks ports. Zimbabwe in southern Africa faced a problem in its export/import sector when it attempted to bypass South Africa's railroad lines to facilitate international trade. The alternate railroad lines were quite difficult to use because of wars in the country of Mozambique.

<u>Boundaries (308-312):</u> Historically, frontiers have separated states. A *frontier* is a zone where no state exercises complete political control–a neutral zone. Frontiers were utilized so that two countries would be less likely to have a direct conflict. Frontiers remain only in Antarctica and the Arabian Peninsula. Today, frontiers have been replaced by *boundaries* which are precise linear divisions that separate countries. Boundaries are divided between *physical* and *cultural.* Physical boundaries are where natural features of the Earth serve as borders between two regions. *Mountain* borders can be effective borders if they are difficult to cross. The Andes and the Himalayas both serve as international boundaries. Deserts can also serve to separate states. Like mountains, *deserts* are difficult and troublesome to cross. *Water*–in the form of rivers, lakes, and oceans–serve as boundaries most common among physical boundaries. Oceanic boundaries are difficult because perceptions differ as to the extent of possession of water beyond a country's coast. The law of the sea gives countries twelve nautical miles of ocean as their exclusive territory. *Cultural boundaries* are made by differences in traits such as language and religion. Sometimes, these boundaries are drawn according to *geometric* configurations. For example, the U.S.-Canadian border has a large straight segment 1,300 miles long which runs on the 49 degree North parallel. This line was drawn by compromise. Straight lines are also common in Africa where the European colonial powers carved up the continent. Differences in *religion* also determine the outlay of boundaries. Northern Ireland and South Asia are good examples of this type of division where Catholics were disconnected from Protestants and Hindus were isolated from Muslims. After World War I, *language* was the main criterion used to designate new countries in post-war Europe. These changes lasted, for the most part, until the 1990's when ethnic conflicts devastated the geographical boundaries of Eastern Europe.

<u>Cyprus and South Africa (312-317):</u> Even though nation-states attempt to use one nationality to establish themselves, often more than one nationality exists in a given state. A state with more than one nationality is a *multinational state*. *Cyprus* is the third largest island in the Mediterranean; it is divided between *Turkish* and *Greek* residents. In 1974 a move by the Greek majority to unify with Greece brought an invasion by the Turks to protect the Turkish minority. The resulting compromise has divided the island into two parts, one for the Turks and the other for the Greeks. A buffer zone patrolled by UN soldiers assures there is little contact between the two groups. South Africa is another country consisting of several ethnic groups. The first Europeans to settle South Africa were *Boers*, so-named for their dialect from Holland. Britain ruled the country entirely between 1902 and 1948, when it reverted back to the hands of the Boers. Afraid of the black majority, the Boers (also Afrikaners) created *apartheid*, which was a legal system that kept blacks and whites segregated into different geographical areas. Blacks were only allowed low-paying jobs while whites were allotted better jobs, housing, and opportunity. Blacks were herded into *"homelands"* that had little utility in agriculture. Many countries reacted to these policies by severing relations with South Africa as a form of protest to their policies. In 1991, the white-dominating government of South Africa repealed apartheid laws, freed imprisoned leader *Nelson Mandela*, and legalized the *African National Congress* (the anti-apartheid political group).

The Former Soviet Union (317-320): The early 1990's has been witness to the former Soviet Union's break up. Cultures within the former country have sought self-rule during the last few years. The Baltic states of *Estonia, Latvia, and Lithuania* became independent from Russia because of their historical roots and the fact their culture is different from that of Russians. *Belarus* and *Ukraine* are distinctly different from Russians for they have been separated from Russia for 500 years of their history due to foreign domination. Time allowed them to develop distinct cultural differences. The Crimean Peninsula is also a part of Ukraine, which is populated largely by Russians. The Russian government officially recognizes *39 nationalities* within its borders. They are spread throughout central Russia. One problem the Russian government faces is suppressing independence movements by these groups. The *Chechnyans* began fighting a war of independence with the Russians in 1994 after the Russian Army was sent to placate the Chechnyans. Russians living in countries that were former republics in the Soviet Union have found they are now subject to discrimination because the tables of population have turned, changing them into a minority.

One Nationality in More Than One State (320-325): Conflicts sometime develop when the population of a group is spread over more than one state. Unrest is often the result of nationalities and states. Africa has had many bouts of wars and hostilities between ethnic groups who have fought over national boundaries. Historically, much of Africa was occupied by tribes rather than states, though in West Africa there have been some Kingdoms. When the Europeans drew the national boundaries in Africa, little attention was paid to traditional tribal areas. Consequently, hostilities have erupted over territorial disagreements because each nation-state is home to many different ethnic groups. The *Caucasus* region of the former Soviet Union (between the Black and Caspian seas) is home to many different nationalities. The *Azeris* were a group living in this mountainous area. A treaty in 1828 gave half of their territory to Persia and half to Russia. Now six million people live in bothh Iran and the newly formed country of Azerbaijan. *Armenians* are an ethnic group who populate much of the Caucasus. They were forced to emigrate from Russia and Turkey. The Turks killed hundred of thousands of Armenians during the late 19th and early 20th centuries. Armenia became an independent country in 1991, and has since been waging a border dispute with Azerbaijan. *Georgia* is another new country to rise from the former U.S.S.R.. Its majority is only 69 percent of the overall population. The *Kurd* people live south of Armenia and Azerbaijan. Their population of 10 million is spread throughout Iran, Iraq, and Turkey. Although the European allies made a state for Kurds following their World War I victory, it was swallowed up by Turkey soon after. Ever since, Kurds have been suppressed by the Turks. The Kurds have waged a guerrilla war against Turkey since 1984. Kurds have also fared poorly in Iran and Iraq.

The Balkans (325-328): After World War I, the country of Yugoslavia was born and united the six republics into one, unified country. Yugoslavia has suffered from war since the break up of the former country into six independent states. The main reason for these disputes has been border conflicts. Each country such as the Serbs or Croats seek to gain territory that they see for historical or other reasons as their own legitimate land.

Balkanization is the term used to describe the breakdown of a state through internal disputes among its different nationalities.

Internal Organization of States (329-331): A ***unitary state*** places power into the hands of a central government. Unitary governments are more common in smaller countries which have few internal differences. Sometimes unitary systems are used where many ethnic groups exist so that one culture may be imposed upon other members of society. ***Federal*** states allocate substantial power to smaller units of government within the nation-state. Most of the world's largest states are federal, including the U.S., Canada, Russia, and Brazil. The trend of late has been to decentralize government. For example, ***France*** granted more power to its departments and communes, allowing them to be responsible for their own internal affairs. ***Poland*** has also switched to a federalized system of government because the former unitarian regime allowed buildings, roads, and water systems to deteriorate greatly. Poland is now divided into 2,400 municipalities; each is given the option of running various parts of their government or allowing the federal government to do so. Many former government employees were rejected from jobs because of their affiliation with the old communist regime.

Political and Military Cooperation (331-332): The largest international organization is the ***United Nations*** which has grown from 49 states in 1945 to 185 in the early 1990's. Many members were added in 1955 from countries liberated from Nazi Germany, in 1960 from newly independent African countries, and in 1990 from newly emancipated countries from the former U.S.S.R.. The United Nations can be used for peace-keeping forces in other countries. The UN has been used to perform this function in the Persian Gulf, Bosnia-Hercegovina, and Somalia during the 1990's.

Two Superpowers (332-336): During the Napoleonic Wars of the early 1800's, there were eight dominant powers in the world. The same number existed by the outbreak of World War I. When there were so many powerful nations that were allied equally the condition of a balance of power existed. However, by the end of World War II, the ***U.S.*** and ***Soviet Union*** alone were much more powerful than all other nations on Earth. They were ***superpowers***. When allies threatened to tip the scales of power in favor of the other superpower, military intervention often ensued. For example, the Soviet Union sent troops into ***Czechoslovakia*** in 1968 and ***Afghanistan*** in 1979 to install Soviet-friendly governments. The U.S. has also deployed troops to the ***Dominican Republic*** in 1965 and to ***Panama*** in 1989 to ensure their governments would remain U.S. allies. Both countries also installed military bases in strategic points around the globe. The ***North Atlantic Treaty Organization (NATO)*** was formed to create a cohesive military bloc headed by the U.S., Canada, and democratic European countries. The ***Warsaw Pact*** allied Eastern European countries together to combat any possible invasion by countries lying outside of the agreement. Western Hemisphere countries convene in the ***Organization of American State (OAS)***. The OAS promotes social, cultural, political, and economic ties between member countries. In Africa the ***Organization for African Unity (OAU)*** performs a similar function. Former British colonies are organized into the Commonwealth of

Nations. The ***Nonaligned Movement*** includes nearly every country in Africa and the Middle East.

Economic Cooperation (336-339): European states have increasingly looked to better their economic cooperation. The ***European Union*** is the vehicle by which this is being achieved. This is a common market that increases intraregional trade between member countries by using tariff reduction policies to increase trade in the region. The European Union has also worked to increase living standards in poorer areas such as southern Italy. The most dominant country in Western Europe is ***Germany***. Even after its defeat in World War II, Germany has emerged as the strongest economy in the European Union. Many of its neighbors have become worried about the strength which Germany possesses, and when history is observed they may have need to be. Since the liberation of Eastern Europe from Communism, many of its member countries desire to become members of the European Union. However, current member countries are hesitant to allow this because the addition of so many poorer countries would likely drain some money from the richer, established countries of the European Union.

The Future Economy of Europe (340-341): As Europeans tear down the boundaries that have separated them for centuries, interesting problems arise. For example, the large number of different languages is a large drain on the bureaucracy's budget due to translation costs. Different prices in countries bring about a very integrated economy in which nationals of one country may buy up property as the Germans do in France. Interestingly, many Europeans in Western Europe have resisted the immigration to their countries of immigrants, seen as an economic and criminal threat. Additionally, the ***rates of natural increase*** of many Asian and African immigrants is quite high which, in the long term, will cause the indigenous Europeans to become a smaller percentage of the overall population.

CLOSING REMARKS

A state is a political unit encompassing all peoples within its borders, whereas a nation is a group of people who well may reside in part or all of one state or more than one state. Boundaries are drawn because of physical and cultural influences. In some parts of the world, such as Western Europe, boundaries have become less important because of economic maturity; but in Eastern Europe ethnic nationalism has lead to the erection of borders to keep other ethnic groups from entering. When perceptions of proper border locations vary greatly, war often erupts in places like the former Yugoslavia and in India-Pakistan.

KEY TERMS AND CONCEPTS

Globalization: The transference of military, economic, and political power to a regional authority. The European Union is a good example.

Cultural Diversity: Increases in the number of groups competing for more political control over the states which they populate.

State: An area organized into a political unit and ruled by an established government with control over its internal and foreign affairs. The U.S. is a state.

Sovereignty: Ability of a state to govern its territory free from control of its internal affairs by other states. When the U.S. broke from Great Britain, it attained sovereignty.

City-state: A sovereign state that comprises a town and surrounding countryside. San Marino and the Vatican are modern versions of this.

Colony: A territory that is legally tied to a sovereign state rather than completely independent. The U.S. was founded using thirteen original British colonies.

Colonialism: Attempt by one country to establish settlements and to impose its political, economic, and cultural principles in another territory. Great Britain was the largest colonial power in the last three centuries.

Nationality (Nation): A group of people who occupy a particular area and have a strong sense of unity based on a set of shared beliefs and attitudes. The Kurds of Asia are a strong example.

Self-determination: Concept that nationalities have the right to govern themselves. This increasingly becomes a factor when states have many nationalities within their borders.

Nation-state: A state whose territory corresponds to that occupied by a particular nation. Denmark is a good example.

Centripetal forces: Attitudes that tend to unify a people and enhance support for the state. Forces that bring people together around their core.

Nationalism: Attitude of the people in a nation in support of the existence and growth of a particular state. Nazi Germany is where nationalism was greatly emphasized.

Boundary: Invisible line that marks the extent of territory. They are formed by physical and cultural influences.

Compact state: A state in which the distance from the center to any boundary does not vary significantly. Nearly circular shaped states represent this form of state.

Prorupted state: An otherwise compact state with a large projecting extension. The extension serves either to give access to a geographic feature or to act as a geographical barrier to other states.

Elongated state: A state with a long, narrow shape. Communication and transportation to their far reaches are often difficult.

Fragmented state: A state that includes several discontinuous pieces of territory. The U.S. is such as state because of outlying Alaska and Hawaii.

Perforated state: A state that completely surrounds another one. South Africa completely surrounds Lesotho, making it such a state.

Landlocked state: A state which has no outlet to the sea. In South America, Paraguay and Bolivia are both landlocked.

Frontier: A zone separating two states in which neither state exercises political control. In the past, such zones were prominent but in today's world they are very rare. *Antartica*

Multinational state: A state that contains more than one nationality. The U.S. is very much an example of this type of state.

Apartheid: Laws (no longer in effect) in South Africa that physically separated different races into different geographic areas. In 1991, apartheid in South Africa ceased to legally exist.

Balkanized: Small geographic area that can not be successfully organized into one or more stable states because it is inhabited by many nationalities with complex, long-standing antagonisms toward each other.

Balkanization: Process by which a state breaks down through conflicts among its nationalities. The former U.S.S.R. is a good example.

Unitary state: An internal organization of a state that places most power in the hands of central government officials. The former Soviet Union had this form of government.

Federal state: An internal organization of a state that allocates most powers to units of local government. The U.S. does this in the political sub-units of states.

Balance of Power: Condition of roughly equal strength between opposing countries or alliances of countries. Today, the U.S. tips any alliance because it is a superpower, far more powerful than any other country on Earth.

CHAPTER SEVEN

1. An area organized into a political unit is called a _____.   state

2. The largest state in the world in terms of _____ is Russia, while   area
China is in terms of _____.   population

3. The term state is synonymous with _____.   country

4. Globalization is a political trend in which authority is _____ to   transferred
a regional authority.

5. Pressure caused by individual cultural groups to gain more
political power is called _____ _____.   cultural diversity

6. Independence from control of a state's internal affairs is _____.   sovereignty

7. _____ was a Japanese colony until it was divided into two parts   Korea
following World War II.

8. The continent of _____ is territory not populated and is not   Antarctica
part of a _____ state.   sovereign

9. The nationalists lost a civil war in _____, and left to establish a   China
government of the island of _____.   Taiwan

10. Ancient _____ lasted from about 3000 B.C. until it was   Egypt
conquered by the Romans in the fifth century A.D..

11. Great Britain established many _____ in many parts of the   colonies
world which added to its economic _____.   base

12. The most populous remaining colony in the world is _____   Hong
_____, which will revert to _____ control in 1997.   Kong, Chinese

13. Most colonial powers were from the continent of _____.   Europe

14. A _____ is a collection of people who share a common   nation
culture and history who may live in _____ than one country.   more

15. The concept that nationalities have the right to govern
themselves is _____-_____.   self-determination

16. The boundaries of states _____ correspond to the boundaries of nations.

rarely

17. _____ annexed the _____ in the 1930's because the majority of its population spoke German.

Germany, Sudetenland

18. When people retain a high degree of loyalty and devotion to their home state they are said to possess a high degree of _____.

nationalism

19. During the early 1990's, a resurgence of nationalism occurred in _____ _____.

Eastern Europe

20. Territory is liminted in extent by _____.

boundaries

21. Due to its shape, Chile is called an _____ state.

elongated

22. States which have discontinuous territory are labeled _____ states.

fragmented

23. Lesotho is a _____ state, surrounded by the country of _____ _____.

landlocked, South Africa

24. Zones in which no state exercises complete control are known as _____.

frontiers

25. Three physical elements that act as boundaries are _____, _____ and _____.

mountain, deserts water

26. A _____ boundary separates Chile from Argentina in South America.

mountain

27. After colonial rule ended in most of its countries (shortly after World War II) _____ was divided by geometric lines with little national correspondence.

Africa

28. _____ states contain more than one nationality.

Mulitnational

29. The island of _____ in the Mediterranean Sea is divided between Greek and _____ nationalities.

Cyprus
Turkish

30. Physical separation of people based on race was called _____ in South Africa.

apartheid

31. _____, _____, and _____ are new republics situated on the shores of the Baltic Sea.

Estonia, Latvia, Lithuania

32. The process by which a state breaks down due to conflict among its different nationalities is called _____.

Balkinization

33. _____ states allocate political power to local units of government within a country.

Federal

34. The country of Poland has switched from a _____ form of government to a _____ system of government after communism in Poland lost power.

unitary
federal

35. Equal strength among opposing allies is called a _____ of _____.

balance,
power

36. The country of _____ has come to dominate the other countries of Western Europe in economic and political power.

Germany

CHAPTER EIGHT

DEVELOPMENT

OVERVIEW

Chapter Eight gives an overview of development and how it has been achieved in different parts of the world. In most of the world's homes, people live without many of the comforts taken for granted in the Western world. People in many places on Earth live without good streets, water systems, education, or health care. The standard-of-living gap between poorer countries (LDC's) and richer countries (MDC's) continues to grow larger. In an effort to increase their living standards, LDC governments attempt to embrace the concept of economic development.

SELECTED NOTES

Fundamentals of Development (349-350): The population of the world can be roughly divided into groups of relatively rich and relatively poor peoples. Due to world-wide spatial variations in natural resources, economic policy, culture, and technology, some places, such as the U.S. and Japan, have developed strong economies, while other regions, such as Latin America and Africa, have not kept pace economically. One factor restricting economic improvement is low status of women burdened by low-level education and numerous children. *Development* is the process of improving the material conditions of people through diffusion of knowledge and technology. *Economic development* is a continuous, never-ending process to improve the health and prosperity of the people. States which are in more mature stages of economic development are called *more developed countries (MDC's)*, while countries that have not progressed far economically are dubbed *less developed countries (LDC's)*. Developing countries is another term used to refer to LDC's. Geographically, LDC's are found in clusters, as are MDC's. These clusters occur because many of the ingredients for economic success (culture, resources) cross boundaries in certain regions. In general, the 30 degree North parallel divides many MDC's situated north of that line from the LDC's found south of that line of latitude; it is known as the *north-south split*.

Indicators of Development (350-352): Economic, social, and demographic traits mark a country's level of development. In MDC's people tend to have a higher per capita income because they are more apt to work in a more balanced economy in which job yields are higher than in a very restricted economy. Because of higher levels of wealth, people in MDC's can purchase more goods which, in turn, can support more people financially. The populations of MDC's tend to have better health, higher levels of education, more forms of communication, and better infrastructures than countries labeled LDC's.

Per Capita Income and Economic Structure (352-354): The **gross domestic product (GDP)** of a country is the value of its total output of goods and services in a given year. By dividing this value by the population of a country, the **per capita gross domestic product** may be found. In most LDC's the per capita GDP is less than $1,000 per year, while in MDC's most countries it exceeds $15,000 annually. **Switzerland** has the world's highest per capita GDP at over $30,000. The gap in per capita GDP between MDC's and LDC's is expanding. Although per capita GDP is the mean income for a state's population, it can be misleading if the disparity of income within a country is great. Economies are generally divided into three segments–Primary, Secondary, and Tertiary. **1-Primary sector** includes the harvest of raw materials such as mining, agriculture, fishing, and forestry. **2-Secondary** includes manufacturing of raw materials into goods. **3-Tertiary** includes the providing of goods and services directly to consumers. In most LDC's agriculture dominates; food consumption is of paramount importance. However, as one progresses to richer and richer countries, agriculture becomes more efficient and/or the other two sectors are better capable of providing jobs and incomes. In MDC's the tertiary sector has become more prevalent in recent years, as manufacturing has decreased and has been restructured into three branches. In restructured mode: **3-Tertiary sector** includes transportation, communications, and utilities. **4-Quaternary sector** includes business services such as trade, insurance, banking, advertising and wholesaling. Finally, **5-Quinary sector** includes services in health, education, research, government, retail, tourism, and recreation.

Worker Productivity and Raw Material Access (354-355): **Productivity** is the value of a particular product compared to the amount of labor needed to make it. **Value added** is the gross value of a product after manufacturing minus the costs of raw materials and energy. Both productivity and value added are much greater in MDC's than in LDC's. Raw materials are essential to the economic development of a country. Minerals and trees which can be altered with energy from coal, petroleum, uranium, and natural gas help to give an economy a strong base with which to work. European countries ran short of many of these materials, so they sought them by colonizing other places in the world. The U.S. and former Soviet Union evolved into powerful nations in part because they possessed many important resources. Some countries, such as Switzerland and Japan, are very advanced owing to their mastery of international trade.

Availability of Consumer Goods (355-357): Some wealth generated by MDC's is used for **essential** goods and services (food, clothing and shelter) and the remainder for **non-essential** goods and services (cars, telephones and entertainment). By expanding the number of non-essential goods traded, a country may establish a new niche industry that will compliment and strengthen the existing economy. Non-essential goods are much more prevalent in MDC's than in LDC's. Because of the MDC's higher exposure to urban lifestyles, their members often develop cultural identities which are integrally linked with non-essential goods and services such as the telephone, computer, and car.

<u>Social Indicators of Development (357-360):</u> MDC's tend to have significantly higher levels of education than LDC's. In MDC's students attend school longer, have better access to instructors, and include a higher percentage of females. ***Literacy rate*** is the percentage of the country's people who can read and write. Literacy rates exceed 95 percent in MDC's but are less than one-third in many LDC's. In LDC's women receive much less education than do their male counter parts. Because MDC's can afford more and better health treatments, MDC populations are healthier than populations of LDC's. In many MDC's financial support is given to the sick, elderly, orphaned, and veterans. However, due to slow-downs in economic growth, MDC's are having to cut the amount of available public assistance.

<u>Demographic Indicators of Development (360-361):</u> The ***infant mortality rate*** is the number of babies who die during their first year of life per 1,000 born. In MDC's this figure is less than 10 per 1,000, but in many developing countries this figure approaches 100 per 1,000 infants born. Natural increase rates are often higher than two percent in less developed countries, but are ordinarily less than one percent in more developed countries. High rates of natural increase hinder a country from faster per capita economic development. Birth rates high enough to induce higher rates of natural increase are also more common in LDC's because there is usually more pressure placed on women to have many children and birth control is not as readily available. High birth rates in LCD's contribute to a much younger population than in MDC's.

<u>India and the U.S. (361-362):</u> A comparison of the U.S. and India reveals the U.S. has lower rates of increase, more wealth per capita, more raw materials, higher literacy rates, and more non-essential consumer products than does India. These indicators allow geographers to divide the world into MDC's and LDC's, which can be measured by using various economic, social, and demographic terms.

<u>More Developed Regions; Anglo-America and Western Europe (362-365):</u> The ***human development index (HDI)*** is a formula used to indicate the relative level of development a country may have. In 1993, Japan had the highest HDI in the world. Western Europe and Anglo-America have HDI's over .9 on a scale of 0 to 1. Canada and the U.S. make up Anglo-America and have the high ranking of .98 on the HDI. Anglo America is the world's most important food exporter and is, paradoxically, home to the world's largest area of unused farm land. Most of the people are Protestant, and nearly everyone speaks the same English language. Global competition has slowed parts of Anglo-America's economy in recent years. Western Europe's core area of western Germany, northeastern France, northern Italy, Switzerland, Belgium, and the Netherlands retain very high income levels while the peripheral areas have comparatively lower standards of living. Because of low rates of natural increase, immigration from Asia and Africa is a very important factor in Western European development.

<u>Eastern Europe (365-367):</u> Eastern Europe was controlled for forty-five years following World War II by Soviet-influenced centralized planning. Consequently, their economies

were molded by government officials instead of business entrepreneurs. The governments of Eastern European countries would set a series of goals every five years. Soviet planners emphasized heavy industry, a spatially dispersed industrial base, and factories located near raw material sources rather than near potential markets. By some measures Eastern European economies developed well during the 1950's and 1960's. However, by other measures they did not. Communism in Eastern Europe fell in the late 1980's and early 1990's because it had proven disastrous for their economies. Industries were very inefficient, they were environmentally polluting, and their products were not competitive with those found in Western countries. Additionally, Eastern Europe failed to produce sufficient numbers of nonessential consumer goods. After the collapse of Communism, many government factories were privatized, some by foreign corporations. As market economy strategies become more the norm in Eastern Europe, they should begin to economically resemble their Western European neighbors in coming years.

South Pacific, South Africa, and Japan (367-368): These areas are relatively developed. The *South Pacific's* population is dominated by Australia and New Zealand; they comprise over 90 percent of the area's people. Both are net exporters of food and have a good raw materials base in comparison to their small populations. Development in *South Africa* is higher than in any other African nation. Still, apartheid has dampened the economic successes of this state. Although the *Japanese* are remote and endowed with few resources and relatively little farm land, they have emerged as the most developed nation in the world, according to the UN. Strong education and superior marketing not discouraged by the government have allowed Japan to specialize in high-end consumer products that have placed it at the top of the world's developed countries.

Latin America (368-369): Latin America is considered a less developed region. Overall, Latinos tend to be Spanish- or Portuguese-speaking, Catholic, and more likely to inhabit cities than the countryside. In South America the population tends to be concentrated along the coast in cities and sparse in much of its interior. The area does have very large inequities in income distribution.

East Asia (369-370): *China* is the most populous country in the world, but ranks among the world's poorest. Historically, Chinese farmers were controlled by property owners who took a large share of their harvests and charged their tenants high rents. In 1949, the Communists won the revolution and instituted new policies on land reform. In recent years government control has loosened somewhat, allowing farmers more control over their crops.

Southeast Asia (370): The mainland and island countries of Southeast Asia are very hot, they receive abundant rainfall, and they generally have poor soils, with the notable exception of volcanic soils found in places like the island of Java. Rice is the staple crop of the region. The most populous country in the region is the island country of Indonesia. Most of Indonesia's population lives on the island of Java. The Southeast Asian region has very large supplies of tin and some oil reserves. Warfare ravaged the area for fifty years earlier in this century.

The Middle East and South Asia (371-372): Environmentally, the **Middle East** doesn't sustain extensive plant or animal life. However, petroleum discovered below the surface of this largely desert area has ignited an economy that actually has a trade surplus. There are large income disparities in the region, since oil isn't found in plentiful amounts in all countries in the area. Adherence to Islam often can hinder economic development in some economic sectors. Warfare has erupted not only between Jews and Arabs but internally between Arab countries, draining resources from other projects. **South Asia** has a huge population that is dominated by India. Although the region does possess some very good resources, its enormous population dilutes their positive economic impact. South Asian food crops generally do well; dry years of the monsoon cause hardship among its people.

Sub-Saharan Africa (372-374): This enormous area has a large population which is ill-suited to provide food stuffs for its inhabitants. One of the poorest regions in the world, its prospects for economic development are the worst in the world. Poor infrastructures, poor leadership, and wide-spread corruption do not increase its chances for economic development.

Development Through International Trade (374-375): In order for a country to upgrade its economy and wealth it must first identify industries in which it would be competitive and then enter those industries. **W. W. Rostow** developed a five-stage model of economic growth needed for countries to mature economically. The steps numbered one (almost void of consumer goods) to five (widely produced consumer goods), and represent different stages of economic maturity. According to Rostow, all countries are in one of the five stages of development. Countries exposed longer to international trade benefit most from the experience by adjusting their economies accordingly.

States Who've Adopted International Trade (375-376): The petroleum-rich countries of the **Persian Gulf** have successfully adopted the practices of international trade. By exporting oil, they produce monies to finance good economic infrastructures for their companies. Still, the presence of Islam has been an obstacle to Western business practices. South Korea, Taiwan, Singapore, and Hong Kong are nations successful in adjusting to the international trade environment. Their successes have helped them earn the nickname **"The Four Asian Tigers/Dragons."** Even though many states have increased their GDP's by implementing policies that encourage international trade, uneven distribution of resources and frequent market stagnation have blocked continued growth of untapped markets.

Development Through Self-Sufficiency (376-378): The self-sufficiency approach to developing economies suggests a country should spread investment throughout all sectors of its economy, rather than concentrate on sectors for which it has a particular advantage. The goal is to achieve a balanced growth in the economy. States that promote a self-sufficiency type of economic policy want to decrease the ability and influence of foreign firms in their countries. **China** and **India** have advocated this policy for many years. However, due to high costs of goods produced under this policy, self-sufficient models are becoming less popular as countries reduce tariffs and encourage international trade. The two main problems with these models are *1-inefficiencies* caused by state firms not having to compete with other firms, and *2-costly bureaucracies* that often are corrupted and abused by business.

Financing Economic Development (378): Poor LDC's most critical obstacle to economic development is a lack of funding. In order to gain funding, LDC's must look to MDC's to help provide financing for infrastructures that will facilitate investment. Water systems, roads, housing, flood controls, and other large-scale projects are imperative to LDC's ability to lure investment. When LDC's acquire aid through loans, they are often unable to repay even the interest on the loan, and are rarely able to pay the entire principle. The populations of LDC's are the majority of the people on Earth, and they angrily ask for and expect economic equality in funding from the MDC's.

CLOSING REMARKS

Development is measured by the attainment of material goods by a state, as reflected by demographic information on education, health, income, and age. In recent years many poor countries in the world have gained population, but their economies have not kept-pace. Poorer countries' main channel toward development lies through borrowing money from MDC's to finance infrastructure improvements. Non-payment on such loans has caused considerable tension between MDC's and LDC's.

KEY TERMS AND CONCEPTS

Development: A process of improvement in the material conditions of people through diffusion and application of knowledge and technology. Countries in latter stages of development have more material goods and services than do those in earlier stages.

Developed Country (Relatively Developed Country, More Developed Country, MDC): A country that has progressed relatively far along a continuum of economic development.

Less Developed Country (Developing Country, LDC): A country that is at a relatively early stage in the process of economic development. LDC's dominate in Africa and Latin America.

Productivity: The value of a particular product compared to the amount of labor needed to make it. MDC's have much higher productivity than do LDC's.

Gross Domestic Product (GDP): The value of the total output of goods and services produced in a country in a given time period, normally one year. MDC's have high GDP's while LDC's have low GDP's.

Primary Sector: The portion of the economy concerned with the direct extraction of materials from Earth's surface, mostly through agriculture but also through mining, fishing, and forestry. LDC's have large primary sectors.

Secondary Sector: The portion of the economy concerned with manufacturing useful products through processing, transforming, and assembling raw materials. LDC's are becoming more competitive in secondary sectors.

Tertiary Sector: The portion of the economy concerned with transportation, communications, and utilities, sometimes extended to the provision of all goods and services to people in exchange for payment. It is the largest sector in the U.S. and many of the most developed countries.

Quaternary Sector: The portion of the economy concerned with business services, such as trade, insurance, banking, advertising, and wholesaling.

Quinary Sector: The portion of the economy concerned with health, education, research, government, retailing, tourism, and recreation.

Value Added: The gross value of the product minus the costs of raw materials and energy. Value added is much greater per worker in MDC's than in LDC's.

Non-essential Goods: Products such as cars, entertainment, and telephones not imperative for survival. However, their production greatly compliments an economy.

Literacy Rate: The percentage of a country's people who can read and write. MDC's develop and retain high rates of literacy in their populations.

Human Development Index (HDI): A rating system between 0 and 1 which appraises the countries of the world based upon their living standards. Japan had the highest ranking in 1993.

CHAPTER EIGHT   <u>Progressive Review</u>

1. Most of the world's population live in relatively _____   poor
countries.

2. In LDC's the _____ gender is universally less educated than   female
their _____ counter parts.   male

3. _____ developed countries are home to most of the planet's   Less
population, though (in terms of relative development) they lag
farther and farther behind.

4. _____ is the process of improving the material conditions of   Development
people.

5. Developing countries often do not have a large base of _____   natural
resources with which to develop their _____.   economies

6. The global pattern of LDC's and MDC's can be divided by
using the _____ degree _____ parallel as a partition.   30, North

7. The _____ sector dominates MDC's such as the U.S..   tertiary

8. Productivity is much greater in _____ developed countries than   more
in _____ developed countries.   less

9. Per capita _____ _____ _____ measures the average input into   gross domestic product
the economy by each country's citizens.

10. The country with the highest per capita GDP in the world is
_____.   Switzerland

11. Agriculture, fishing, and mining are part of the _____ sector,   primary
which prevails in _____ developed countries.   less

12. _____ countries colonized overseas areas in the 19th century,   European
and gained access to many raw materials.

13. An LDC such as Bangladesh has _____ telephones per   fewer
hundred people than does an MDC such as Britain.

14. The _____ rate is the percentage of people in a country   literacy
capable of reading and _____.   writing

15. Because their populations tend to have many children per family, _____ developed countries also have _____ age structures than do _____ developed countries.

less, younger
more

16. The UN's measure of development is called the _____ _____ _____.

Human Development Index

17. _____ has the highest rating in the Human Development Index.

Japan

18. Government spending in the U.S. on _____ welfare and _____ programs is a large strain on the U.S. budget.

social, military

19. After World War II, The _____ Curtain divided Europe between market economies and _____ economies.

Iron
communist

20. Communist countries had _____ planned economies which often employed _____-year plans detailing various goals.

centrally
five

21. _____'s economy was jump-started after World War II by an abundant labor force which manufactured low-end goods cheaper than other countries.

Japan

22. _____ _____ is dominated linguistically by Spanish and Portuguese.

Latin America

23. Most Latin Americans prefer to live in _____ , rather than _____, settings.

urban,
rural

24. In 1949, the _____ won China's civil war and instituted new economic policies.

Communists

25. _____ was the principal beneficiary of the Green Revolution.

India

26. W. W. _____ developed a _____-stage model for tracking and plotting economic development through _____ _____.

Rostow, five
international trade

27. The Four Asian Dragons/Tigers include the countries of _____ _____ , _____, _____ _____, and Singapore.

South Korea
Taiwan, Hong Kong

28. _____ and _____ tried for many years to implement self-sufficient economic models.

China, India

29. Although self-sufficient economic models are somewhat balanced, they are _____ due to the large _____ which run them.

inefficient, bureaucracies

30. The Grameen Bank of _____ makes loans to women entrepreneurs.

Bangladesh

CHAPTER NINE

AGRICULTURE

OVERVIEW

Before societies developed technology that spurred exploration, they developed agricultural practices providing them with ample food stuffs. Chapter Nine details the origin of farming as well as the regional differences found throughout the world. The size and output of a region's farms can indicate the general level of development found in that area. Additionally, with populations on Earth continuing to grow (since many countries have not reached the last stage of the demographic transition), even more food will need to be produced in coming years.

SELECTED NOTES

Kansas versus Pakistan (388-389): The Iqbel family of Pakistan grows wheat on a 2.5 acre plot of land. Its harvests in good years will feed the family as well as provide some surplus income with which to purchase other food stuffs or household items. Half way around the planet in Kansas, U.S.A the McKinley's farm encompasses 500 acres. Nearly their entire crop will be sold to processors of grain for income. Two-thirds of the world's people are farmers; the size, production, and operation of their farms vary greatly.

How Did Agriculture Begin? (389-390): *Agriculture* is the modification of the Earth's surface through cultivation of plants and rearing of animals to obtain sustenance or economic gain. A *crop* is any plant cultivated by people. Before organized agriculture, people collected plants and animals as they naturally appeared on the landscape through hunting and gathering. Ordinarily, men hunted animals and women gathered plants. Today, some *250,000* people employ hunting and gathering as their primary means of survival. They live in Africa, Australia, South America, and the Arctic. Through generations, people observed that seeds they threw away reappeared, especially near watered and manured areas. Vegetative planting and seed agriculture are the two main types of plant cultivation. The cutting of stems and dividing of roots and subsequent planting is *vegetative planting* (which happened first); *seed agriculture* (more prominent today) is the planting of seeds resulting from fertilization.

Where Did Agriculture Originate? (390-392): Different agricultural techniques each emanated from their respective hearths. *Carl Sauer* believed vegetative planting originated in Southeast Asia because the climatic and topographical elements encouraged this technique to be used with such crops as the taro, yam, banana, and palm.

Northwestern South America and West Africa could also have been hearths of vegetative planting. Western India, northern China, and Ethiopia were apparently the first places from which seed planting spread. Many advances were made in Southwest Asia that received its technology from western India, where *wheat* and *barley* were domesticated along with the *first herd animals*. From Southwest Asia seed agriculture spread across Europe and North Africa. In the Western Hemisphere, seed agriculture had two hearths—one in southern Mexico and another in northern Peru. They both grew squash, corn, cotton, and beans; the only domesticated animals were the alpaca, llama, and turkey.

Classifying Agriculture Regions (392-393): Different climates and physical environments determine to a large extent what crops will be grown in specific areas. However, improved communication and transportation have encouraged the diffusion of plants to areas away from their hearths. For example, Old World and New World plants now are seen in opposite sides of the world from their original hearths.

Shifting Cultivation (393-396): Farming which provides food primarily for consumption by a farmer's family is called *subsistence farming*. In some countries subsistence farming is practiced by a large percentage of the population, which sells a small surplus to the government or to townspeople. *Slash and burn* agriculture entails burning the vegetative cover of land and then using the resulting nutrients to grow crops. Other farmers use a plot of land and then let it lie fallow long periods of time. In some areas villagers find a desirable piece of land to farm; they clear the trees and other vegetation from the area by cutting them down and burning the fallen plant cover. The cleared land is called *swidden*. In many areas such swidden can only support plants for three years or less; the nutrients are used up quickly. Crops used in shifting agriculture include rice, corn, millet, sorghum, sugar cane, plantain, and vegetables. Shifting agriculture is predominant in the tropics of South America, Southeast Asia, and Africa. Currently, shifting agriculture uses more land than any other type of agriculture, but its future role may well decline owing to economic development.

Pastoral Nomadism (396-400): Subsistence agriculture based upon herding animals is called *pastoral nomadism*. Such nomads live in arid areas that are ill-suited for agriculture. Only fifteen million people practice pastoral nomadism, sparsely occupying 20 percent of the Earth's land area. From their animals pastoral nomads gain hides, meat, milk, and trading power which, in turn, provides them with tents, clothing, food, and prestige. Goats, sheep, and camels are typically found in the herds of nomads, as well as horses (important to the wanderers of Central Asia). Pastoral nomads do not wander aimlessly across the landscape; they have territorial boundaries which they respect. *Transhumance*, seasonal migration between mountain and lowland pastures, is still practiced by some nomads. Due to competition for land, the pastoral nomads way of life is decreasing. Mining and petroleum companies, governments, and farmers increasingly pressure the nomads to give up their way of life and the land on which they depend.

Intensive Subsistence Agriculture (400-403): *Intensive subsistence agriculture* means that farmers must work their land very intensively to harvest enough food to merely meet their own family's needs. This category of farming is found in the densely populated East, South, and Southeast Asia. Because the population density is so high, farmers have no choice but to produce much food on small plots of land. Consequently, virtually no land is wasted by these farmers, planting crops on every piece of land available. Paths and roads are kept very narrow, so as not to take up land that could be producing food. *Wet rice* is the practice of nursing rice plants in a nursery, and then planting to seedlings in a flooded field in which they grow and mature. A farmer plows the land with the help of oxen or water buffalo and plants rice plants. The field, called a *sawah*, is then flooded with water and regulated by the farmer using irrigation. After they mature, rice plants are harvested by hand with knives; the husks, known as *chaff*, are separated from the seeds. Lighter chaff is blown away by the wind, or *winnowed*. In regions where warm winters are common, some farmers get two harvests per year, *double cropping* the ground by planting rice and wheat or barley in alternating cycles. In climates where water is less common wheat and other grains may be intensively grown. This land is worked primarily by human power. In order to keep from exhausting the soil, crop rotation takes place in which different crops are used in consecutive years so that certain nutrients in the soil are not depleted. In China, the communist government tried to make farmers work in communes. The program was dismantled because the harvests decreased substantially since people preferred to work for themselves as they had for centuries.

Characteristics of Commercial Agriculture (403-406): In the U.S. and Canada, farms are becoming larger and the number of farmers smaller because of advances in technology which allow motorized farming methods to be undertaken. Less than two percent of the U.S. population are farmers, yet they feed the entire country and export to other countries. Since 1900, the amount of farm land has remained almost constant, although some *prime agricultural land* has been lost to suburbs expanding away from city cores. Improvements in technology have greatly increased the capacity of the farmer in the U.S. over the last 200 years. More productive machinery, herbicides, fertilizers, and plant and animal breeds allow farmers to produce more than ever before. Farm sizes have steadily become larger in the U.S., with the average farm occupying *468* acres. U.S. commercial farmers sell their produce to firms specializing in processing it. For example, a farmer may sell harvested wheat to General Mills who, in turn, makes cereal to be sold in the retail market. Businesses that process, package, store, distribute, and retail food products are collectively known as *agribusiness*.

Which Crops to Plant? (406-408): When deciding which crops to plant farmers use site factors (the abilities of the soil to produce certain crops) and situational factors of the land (their relative distances to things such as markets and distributors). The Von Thunen model was designed by a farmer in northern Germany to help farmers decide upon which crops to plant, depending upon the location of the farm land itself. The Von Thunen model heavily weighs two factors in its decision-making process: the cost of the land and the cost of transporting the harvest to market. In order to have a profitable crop, a farmer must be sure the cost of transportation does not outweigh the prices paid to the farmer for the crop. Consequently, perishable crops with high transportation costs are located in concentric rings close to cities (markets), while other goods that are less perishable or are cheaply transported may be grown further from the city, for they are still profitable at such longer distances. So, milk and gardens are located near the city while animal grazing is far-removed. The Von Thunen model can be applied to places and nations outside of Germany; it is a conceptual observation which holds true in most areas which possess agriculture.

Mixed Crop and Livestock Farming (408-409): In mixed crop and livestock farming most of the crops are fed directly to livestock to fatten them for slaughter. Livestock supply farmers with meat as well as manure to fertilize the ground. *Corn* is most often used to feed cattle. By having cattle and crops, farmers may more fully use time throughout the year with fewer hours of inefficient time spent waiting for crops to mature. Such diversity also spreads the risk in business. Farmers often divide their land into fields and then plant different crops in two, three, and four year cycles. Cereal grains, root crops, and rest crops (such as clover) are alternately planted so that the nutrients in the soil are replenished every few years. Sometimes the ground is left fallow for a year or two, which allows it to rest. This method of nutrient preservation is called *crop rotation*. A belt from Ohio to the Dakotas, with Iowa as its core, is the corn belt, where half of the U.S. corn is grown. *Soybeans* are the second most important crop in the U.S.. They are used in many food products such as tofu, and are increasingly used as an ingredient in other food products.

Dairy Farming (409-413): In the Northeast U.S., Southeast Canada, and Northwestern Europe, dairy farming is very important. These areas are also home to large urban populations that consume the milk, cheese, and other products derived from milk. The ring surrounding urban areas from which they receive their stocks of milk is called a *milkshed*. Usually, milksheds radiate no more than thirty miles from a city. Milk produced further away from cities is usually used for the production of cheese, butter, and other products, since this milk stays usable longer than drinking milk. Some countries such as New Zealand devote most of their milk production to cheeses and butter, because their location makes the shipping of drinking milk very difficult, due to the relative isolation of New Zealand from the markets of Europe and North America. However, other places like Great Britain, with a large market base, can devote more dairy resources to milk production. Still, low profitability and excessive workloads are dissolving many dairy farms in the U.S..

Grain Farming (413-414): Grasses such as wheat, corn, oats, and barley produce *grains*. They are a staple component crop on most farms. *Wheat* is primarily used for the manufacture of bread. Wheat has a high price, may be stored for long periods of time, and may be grown profitably in remote regions. Large grain farm operations are found in the U.S., Canada, Australia, Argentina, France, and the United Kingdom. In the U.S., wheat is found in three areas. The *winter wheat* belt is found in Texas, Oklahoma, Kansas, and Colorado. This wheat is dormant in the ground during winter. Farther north is the *spring wheat* belt in the Dakotas, Montana, and Saskatchewan. Because of severe winters wheat must be planted in the spring and harvested in late Autumn. Another important wheat territory is the *Palouse region* of eastern Washington state. The *McCormick reaper* first allowed large scale growing and harvesting of wheat. Today, the *combine* reaps, threshes, and cleans wheat immediately after it is harvested in the field. Wheat is extremely important because it is exported by many people and also is universally consumed.

Livestock Ranching (414-416): *Ranching* is the commercial grazing of livestock over an extensive area. Cattle ranching in the U.S. transcends the economic benefit of livestock, for the popularity of the cowboy and ranching in popular culture is extensive. Columbus brought cattle to the New World on his second voyage. Immigrants from Spain and Portugal began ranching in the Americas, for they were the only Europeans with a tradition of cattle ranching. Due to population growth in the Eastern U.S., cattle became a profitable commodity. Thus, cattle were shipped to *Chicago* from the plains upon which they were fattened and eventually, shipped East as slaughtered meat products. Towns in the Old West such as *Abilene, Kansas* became famous for their reputations as centers of wildness (prostitution, gambling, and gunfights were rampant). The most famous route from the grazing plains of Texas to the railroads of Kansas was the *Chisholm Trail*, which today corresponds roughly with U.S. Route 81. Range wars became common between farmers and ranchers (who wanted to drive their cattle across all land). With the invention of *barbed wire* in 1873, farmers began winning this war, and cattle ranchers eventually settled on their own large plots of land, which were often ill-suited for agriculture. Today, 60 percent of all ranch land is leased from the U.S. government. Herefords breeds imported from England have replaced the Longhorn cattle stocks of the Old West. Cattle are still raised on ranches but regularly sent to farms to be fattened by eating corn.

Cattle Ranching Outside The U.S. (416-417): Europe has few cattle ranches outside of Spain and Portugal. Latin America does have significant cattle operations in southern Brazil, Uruguay, and on the *Pampas* of Argentina. Ranching has declined in Argentina because farming is more profitable. Ranches in the Middle East, Australia, New Zealand, and South Africa tend to have more sheep than cattle on them. Today, many ranching operations are owned by companies in the meat-packing industry.

Mediterranean Agriculture and Truck Farming (417-418): Mediterranean farming takes place in areas bordering the Mediterranean Sea as well as California, Central Chile, and Southwestern Australia. These regions often practice horticulture, which is the growing of fruits, vegetables, and flowers for human consumption. Most of the world's olives, grapes, fruits, and vegetables are grown in these regions. Wine is also produced mainly in these climates from France to California to Chile. *Irrigation* is very important to farming in this climate because precipitation is not plentiful, and tends to come in the winter. Fruits and vegetables are also grown in the U.S.'s Southeast because they help supply the populous Northeast with food. *Truck farmers* take advantage of using machines at every possible opportunity, because they tend to make farming more profitable. Crops that are increasing in demand are strawberries, asparagus, peppers, and mushrooms. Costs are kept down buy hiring undocumented immigrants to perform much of the labor-intensive duties such as harvesting and planting crops by hand.

Plantation Farming (418-419): Plantations are large farms which specialize in one or two crops, and are found primarily in Latin America, Africa, and Asia. They are usually found in sparsely populated areas; therefore, they usually must import, house, and entertain their workers for there are no established communities at which they may do so independently. Today, crops are often processed at the plantation, reducing their bulk and weight, making them cheaper to transport to far-away markets. After the abolition of slavery in the U.S. in 1863, plantations became less important components of the economy of the South.

Subsistence Farmers and Drug Crops (420-421): Large population increases are found in many countries where people farm at subsistence levels. Due to the expanding populations, there is often not enough food to provide for the entire country's populace. If these countries are going to meet the demand for food, they may be forced in the future to switch to more automated modes of agricultural production. Coca leaves which are processed into cocaine originate from South American countries like Peru, Bolivia, Colombia, and Ecuador. Most of the processing and distribution takes place in Colombia. Most of the marijuana imported into the U.S. originates in Mexico, Colombia, and Jamaica. Opium used to manufacture heroin is grown mostly in Asia, though Mexico produces some of this crop also. The sales of such crops brings hard currency into developing countries, though the U.S. pressures countries to destroy drug crops.

Commercial Farming and the U.S. Government Policies (421-422): Commercial farming suffers from lower prices, thus lower profitability because they produce more crops than the U.S. market can absorb. Because of more productive plant breeds, management practices, chemicals, and equipment, production of crops in the U.S. is very high. The result of this efficient production is very low crop prices. In order to soften the impact of low crop prices, the U.S. government *subsidizes* farmers. For example, if a farmer doesn't receive a market price of a certain level, the government pays the difference to the farmer. The government also pays farmers not to grow certain foods that are saturated in the market place. Ironically, the U.S. government attempts to suppress food production while may other governments struggle to increase their food production.

CLOSING REMARKS

The world has a wide variety in types of farming and levels of production of those farms. Some advanced places annually churn out much more food than its population needs, while other less developed countries struggle to feed their expanding populations. More than likely, without widespread modern technology and lower population growth, many LDC's will have to continue to struggle to feed their respective populations.

KEY TERMS AND CONCEPTS

Agriculture: The deliberate effort to modify a portion of Earth's surface through the cultivation of crops and the raising of livestock for sustenance or economic gain. In MDC's fewer people participate in this activity than in the past.

Crop: Grain or fruit gathered from a field as a harvest during a particular season. The harvest is culturally very important to many societies.

Vegetative Planting: Reproduction of plants by direct cloning from existing plants. This is often performed when growing rice plants.

Seed Agriculture: Reproduction of plants through annual introduction of seeds, which result from fertilization. Grain production is initiated using seeds.

Subsistence Agriculture: Agriculture designed primarily to provide food for direct consumption by the farmer and the farmer's family. LDC's widely use subsistence agriculture.

Slash-and-Burn Agriculture: Another name for shifting agriculture, so named because fields are cleared by slashing the vegetation and burning the debris. Its practice has been opposed by many environmentalists.

Swidden: A patch of land cleared for planting through slashing and burning. Rarely are swiddens used for more than three years.

Shifting Cultivation: A form of subsistence agriculture in which people shift activity from one field to another. Each field is used for crops for a relatively few years, and left fallow for long periods.

Pastoral Nomadism: A form of subsistence agriculture based on herding domesticated animals. Pastoral nomadism usually takes place in very arid regions.

Transhumance: The seasonal migration of livestock between mountains and lowland pastures. Transhumance allows for more balance feeding on the land.

Pasture: Grass or other plants grown for feeding grazing animals, as well as land used for grazing. It is important not to overgraze pastors, else erosion will occur.

Intensive Subsistence Agriculture: A form of subsistence agriculture in which farmers must expend a relatively large amount of effort to produce the maximum feasible yield from a small parcel of land. Southeast Asia has much land allocated to this type of production.

Wet Rice: Rice grown for much of the time in deliberately flooded fields. This crop is very important to East Asians and Western Indians.

Sawah: A flooded field for growing rice. Irrigation helps flood the sawah and regulate the water level.

Paddy: Malay word for wet rice. It is often incorrectly used by Westerners to describe Sawahs.

Chaff: Husks of grain separated from the seed by threshing. Usually chaff is discarded by U.S. farmers.

Thresh: Action that beats out grain from stalks by trampling upon it.

Winnow: To remove chaff by allowing it to be blown away by the wind.

Hull: The outer covering of a seed. It is removed by mortar and pestle in rice.

Double Cropping: Harvesting twice a year from the same field. It is difficult to do if the region has a long dry season.

Crop Rotation: The practice of rotating fields from crop to crop each year to avoid exhausting the soil. Nitrogen-injecting crops such as sweet clover are occasionally used to strengthen the soil.

Commercial Agriculture: Agriculture undertaken primarily to generate products for sale off the farm. U.S. farmers mostly belong to this category.

Agribusiness: Commercial agriculture characterized by integration of different steps in the food processing industry, usually through ownership by large corporations.

Prime Agricultural Land: The most productive farmland. In the U.S., much of it is now being used for residential housing construction.

Von Thunen: A German who published "The Isolated State" in 1826, which informed farmers of the best location in which to plant their crops in relation to the nearest city.

Cereal Grain: A grass yielding grain for food. Wheat, barley, and corn are cereal grain.

Milkshed: The area surrounding a city from which milk is supplied. Thirty miles is the general limit for a city's milkshed.

Grain: Seed of a cereal grain. The most valuable part of the harvest, with the chaff and straw being byproducts.

Winter Wheat: Wheat planted in the Fall and harvested in the early Summer. This dominates the Kansas, Colorado, and Oklahoma region.

Spring Wheat: Wheat planted in the spring and harvested in the late summer. Places where harsh winters are common usually plant Spring wheat.

Reaper: A machine that cuts grain standing in the field. Its invention by Cyrus McCormick made wheat production more lucrative.

Combine: A machine that reaps, threshes, and cleans grain while moving over a field. Specialized custom-cutting crews use combines to cut wheat from Texas to Canada during the harvesting season.

Ranching: A form of commercial agriculture in which livestock graze over an extensive area.

Horticulture: The growing of fruits, vegetables, and flowers. These products are meant for human, not animal, consumption.

Truck Farming: Commercial gardening and fruit farming, so-named because truck was a Middle English word meaning bartering or the exchange of commodities.

Plantation: A large farm in tropical and subtropical climates that specializes in the production of one or two crops for sale, usually to a developed country. U.S. plantations declined sharply after the Civil War.

Progressive Review

1. The world "_____" means "to care for."   cultivate

2. Any plant cultivated by people is called a _____.   crop

3. Two-thirds of the people in the world are _____, but less than   farmers
   _____ percent of the U.S. population are farmers.   two

4. 468 acres is the average size of a farm in the _____ _____.   United States

5. Agriculture is deliberate modification of the Earth's surface for
   the rearing of _____ and the growing of _____ .   animals, plants

6. Today, 250,000 people in the world survive by hunting and
   _____.   gathering

7. Two types of cultivation are _____ planting and _____   vegetative, seed
   agriculture.

8. The hearth of vegetative planting is probably in _____ Asia   Southeast
   according to Sauer.

9. In the Western Hemisphere, southern _____ and northern   Mexico, Peru
   _____ were the two hearths of agricultural development.

10. When people use different plots of land each year to plant
    their crops, they use _____ cultivation.   shifting

11. Slash-and-_____ agriculture clears land for planting.   burn

12. Swidden is a name used to describe _____ land.   cleared

13. People who live in arid regions sometimes travel over large
    tracts of land searching for food and water for their livestock, a
    practice called _____ _____.   pastoral nomadism

14. Cassava and Maize were domesticated in the continent of
    _____ _____.   South America

15. The size of a nomad's herd is a sign of _____ and _____ in   power, prestige
    many cultures.

128

16. In Central Asia, the _____ holds much importance to nomadic herders.

horse

17. Today, the number of nomads in the world is _____ because of more intense competition for land.

decreasing

18. To maximize food production, _____ _____ farmers waste virtually no land.

intensive subsistence

19. A flooded field is called a _____, and not a paddy as is often believed.

sawah

20. _____ _____ is grown most easily on flat land for water management is easier performed on level ground.

Wet rice

21. When two harvests are taken in a year, _____ _____ is being practiced.

double cropping

22. After 1949, _____ redesigned its farms around communes which proved ineffective in terms of motivation for the workers.

China

23. _____ agricultural _____ is often expropriated by cities to expand their suburbs.

Prime, land

24. _____ is the system of commercial farming and related industries found in the U.S. and other advanced countries.

Agribusiness

25. _____ factors affect farmers' decision on which crops to plant due to their proximity to a city.

Situational

26. The ring around cities where milk production is found is called a _____.

milkshed

27. Oats, wheat, and barley are called _____ grains.

cereal

28. The second most important agriculture crop in the U.S., due to its wide array of uses, is the _____.

soybean

29. Dairies which produce cheeses and butters are found _____ distances from the cities they supply compared to milk-producing dairies.

long

30. _____ _____ is the world's largest producer of dairy products.

New Zealand

31. Dairies are _____ in number in the U.S. in recent years.   decreasing

32. Today, _____ perform most of the harvesting of wheat in the U.S. and Canada.   combines

33. Kansas and Oklahoma are in the _____ wheat _____.   Winter, belt

34. The invention of _____ _____ in 1873 helped farmers combat the territorial aggressions of ranchers.   barbed wire

35. The _____ Trail was the main cattle drive between Brownsville, Texas and the railways in northern Kansas.   Chisholm

36. Most of the world's wine is produced in the lands adjacent to the _____ Sea.   Mediterranean

37. _____ farming is practiced widely in the U.S. Southeast, and produces many varieties of fruits and vegetables.   Truck

38. _____ leaves are the fundamental ingredient in the manufacture of cocaine.   Coca

39. Most of the marijuana that reaches the U.S. is grown in _____.   Mexico

40. Today, plantations are found mainly in Latin America, _____, and _____.   Africa Asia

CHAPTER 10

INDUSTRY

OVERVIEW

When one observes the origin of products–automobiles, computers, and clothing, as well as the components that form the products–it becomes obvious that countries situated all over Earth's surface play a major part in our everyday life. Mexico, Taiwan, Malaysia, and Italy are just a sample of the nations that can be found labeled onto goods used everywhere in the U.S.. Chapter 10 discusses origins of the industrial revolution, how industry is distributed worldwide, locational influences, and problems that face industry in today's global society. As comparative advantages of different locations become more influential with the dissolution of tariffs that impede international trade, geographical analysis of countries and their territories will help explain and determine locations of future industrial growth.

SELECTED NOTES

Maquiladoras (428): Factories and assembly plants that locate in Mexico to take advantage of inexpensive labor existing there are called *Maquiladoras*. The workers in such plants owned by companies like General Motors, Zenith, Ford, and others make fifty cents per hour, the national minimum wage of Mexico. Currently, over 1,000 U.S. companies operate maquiladoras in Mexico. General Motors alone employs over 25,000 people in its maquiladoras.

General Motors' Saturn Plant (429): In January, 1985 GM announced that it was designing the Saturn model automobile, and was searching for an *ideal location* for plants that would assemble this product. Intense competition between states and cities consequently followed, because of the great economic benefits that would be derived from the plant. *Spring Hill, Tennessee* was chosen for the site after a seven month search. Spring Hill was close to the market, accessible by parts suppliers, and was a good community. In other words, Spring Hill beat out the competition because it was the best *geographic site* for the automobile plant, according to GM decision maters.

The Industrial Revolution (429-430): In *Britain,* during the late 1700's, the industrial revolution was born. Innovations in manufacturing and efficiency that brought forth higher quantities of goods to consumers at higher qualities for lower prices than ever before. Good such as guns, food, tobacco, and textiles were manufactured very efficiently, due to the talents of engineers and managers. Before the industrial revolution, manufacturing was dispersed across the landscape in people's homes in the form of the *cottage industry*. Merchants would contract to home-based workers who would be supplied with materials by *putters-out,* the "middle men" employed by merchants to conduct transactions. The most important example of the technology wrought by the industrial revolution was the *steam engine,* patented by James Watt in 1769 in Glasgow, Scotland; it increased immensely the efficiency of factories.

Diffusion from the Iron Industry (430): The iron industry was the first to benefit from Watt's new invention. Iron ore mined from the ground would be smelted in blast furnaces, poured into casts, then transported for further refinement in the form of pig iron. The usefulness of the steam engine was to keep the furnaces hot during the heating and cooling of the iron and steel during production. Henry Cort developed a new way of purifying iron called puddling, which effectively purified pig iron. Cort and Watt's inventions increased iron-manufacturing capabilities, which directly affected many other key industries.

Coal, Engineering, & Transportation (430-431): Prior to the industrial revolution, the primary source of energy was wood. However in addition to heat, wood was being used for many other purposes such as ship building, construction, and furniture. Wood was becoming scarce. The obvious solution was to switch from wood to *coal* for a source of fuel. The furnaces, forges, and mills scattered throughout Britain became clustered into four large, integrated centers, all situated near coal fields. In 1795, *Watt* and *Matthew Bolson* began their own business, producing hundreds of new machines that greatly increased the efficiency of the industrial process, giving birth to modern engineering. There were transportation inventions in the form of canals and railways. In 1759, the Duke of Bridgewater began construction on a canal between Manchester and Worsley which was completed in two years. The canal allowed goods to be transported inexpensively and quickly. Soon, however, canals were eclipsed by the invention of the railway or "iron horse" invented by *William Symington* and *William Murdoch* in 1784. The railway symbolized the impact of engineering on the industrial revolution. The first public railway ran between Stockton and Darlington in the north of England in 1825.

Textiles and Chemicals (431-432): The textile industry benefited greatly from the industrial revolution. Inventions created between 1760 and 1800 transformed the textile industry into a complex factory system; it had previously been a cottage industry. *Richard Arkwright* improved the process of spinning yarn by patenting the process of *carding*. His factory designs were powered by Watt's steam engine. Cotton clothing had to be bleached and dyed for final production, bringing about the chemical component of the industrial revolution. At first chemicals were used primarily to bleach and dye clothing. As research developed the ability of chemistry to accomplish this task, new uses were found. It was discovered that, by combining natural-fiber cloth such as wool and cotton with various chemicals, new *synthetic* materials could be formed. Today, the largest textile factories in the world are owned by chemical companies.

Food Processing (432): The workers of the industrial revolution could not grow their own food and do their factory jobs. Nicholas Appert developed the canning method in 1810. Although fermenting, drying, and pickling had been acknowledged since ancient times, canning allowed food to be preserved by killing the bacteria that spoil food. The tinned can, invented in 1839 by Peter Durand, made canning cheaper than earlier glass bottling techniques. When it was discovered that calcium chloride, when added to water, reduced its sterilization time, canning increased tenfold in 1861.

Industrial Diffusion from Great Britain (432-434): The Crystal Palace of the 1851 World Fair in London symbolized Britain's dominance in the industrial revolution up to that time. At that time Britain produced half of the world's cotton fabric and iron, and mined two-thirds of its coal. The small island nation had far outpaced the rest of the world. The industrial revolution spread eastward to Europe and westward to the U.S.. Europeans contributed variously to the early efforts of the industrial revolution. For example, the Belgians were coal-mining experts, the Germans made the first industrial cotton gin, and the French had the first coal-fired blast furnace for making iron. Unfortunately, the political disruptions of the **French Revolution** and the **Napoleonic Wars** delayed the spread of the industrial revolution to other European countries until the end of the nineteenth century, when it reached the Netherlands, Russia, and Sweden. They did not catch France, Britain, Belgium, and Germany until the twentieth century. Other southern and eastern European countries joined the industrial revolution later in the twentieth century. The first U.S. textile mill was built in Pawtucket, Rhode Island in 1791 by **Samuel Slater**, a former worker at Arkwright's factory in England. To avoid entanglement in the Napoleonic Wars, the U.S. imposed a trade embargo with Europe in 1808. The embargo sparked domestic industrial development in the U.S.. In the twentieth century industrial technology spread to Canada, Japan, and many former British colonies. However industry remains concentrated in four regions: eastern North America, northwestern Europe, eastern Europe, and Japan (See Figure 10-3).

North America (434-437): Manufacturing in North America is concentrated in the northeastern quadrant; it comprises only five percent of the land area, but accounts for one-third of the population and two-thirds of the industrial output. This area was industrialized partly because it was highly populated, being the principal region from which Europeans settled the U.S. and Canada. Additionally, the raw materials of coal and iron which were essential for development are found here. Within North America several industrialized areas have developed. *1-New England:* The oldest area in the U.S. which specialized in textile manufacturing, due to an abundance of cheap labor. *2-Middle Atlantic:* Located between New York and Washington, industries here take advantage of the large consumer market and the importation of materials through several excellent ports. *3-Mohawk Valley:* Industries that are located along the Hudson River and Erie Canal in upstate New York use cheap electricity from Niagara Falls. *4-Pittsburgh-Lake Erie:* Between Pittsburgh and Cleveland steel is all-important. Ore from Minnesota forms the base for industry here. *5-Western Great Lakes:* Toledo, Detroit, Chicago, and Milwaukee comprise this district. Formed because of its location as a distribution and manufacturing center, these places have great locational advantages for business, especially Chicago. *6-St. Lawrence Valley-Ontario Peninsula:* Canada's most important industrial area. Centrality to the Canadian market and proximity to Niagara Falls (cheap electricity) and the Great Lakes (cheap transportation) enticed business to locate here. In recent times, southeastern states of the U.S. have attracted investment because of right-to-work laws; such laws hamper unions and increase company profits. Los Angeles Seattle, San Diego, and San Francisco on the West coast have also developed many industries in the twentieth century, many of which are supported by government contracts.

Western Europe (437-440): Like the North American manufacturing belt, Western Europe appears as one industrial area but, due to different countries in competition with each other, four distinct regions developed there (See Figure 10-6). *1-The Rhine-Ruhr Valley:* The most important region which stretches from northwestern Germany into parts of Belgium, France, and the Netherlands. Industry here is rather dispersed across the landscape and not concentrated. The Rhine river provides great transportation through most of the region and coal is found in high quantities to stimulate industrial growth. *2-The Mid-Rhine:* This area includes southwestern Germany, northeastern France, and Luxembourg. This area is not home to abundant raw materials, but does have a large population to sustain industry. Frankfurt, Stuttgart, and Mannheim are located here. Frankfort became Germany's financial and commercial center and the hub of its transportation networks. The French portion of this area contains Europe's largest iron ore field which provides two-thirds of France's steel. *3-Great Britain:* The original region of the industrial revolution, most of its industry today is in the south of England at the core of the country's population and wealth. During the twentieth century Britain lost its top global ranking in industry due to global competition from other area's in the world. Their factories tend to be old and out of date. Interestingly, the losers of World War II, Japan and Germany, received financial assistance from the U.S. to build new factories to replace those destroyed by the war; they now lead the world in industrial output, along with the U.S.. *4-Northern Italy:* The Po River Basin of northern Italy has much industry derived from cheap hydro-electricity and cheap labor.

Eastern Europe (440-441): This region is home to seven industrial regions. *1-Central Russian Industrial District:* Russia's oldest district, which doesn't have many natural resources but serves a large population center in and around Moscow. *2-St. Petersburg Industrial District:* An early node of innovation in Eastern Europe. Due to the nearby Baltic Sea, shipping is an industrial base as are textiles, light industrial goods, and chemicals. *3-Eastern Ukraine:* Endowed with generous deposits of coal, iron ore, manganese, and natural gas, this area has many plants which are able utilize these assets. *4-The Volga Industrial District:* The largest oil and natural gas fields in Russia are located here. German occupation during World War II enhanced the industry in this area. *5-The Urals Industrial District:* Although this area is home to more than 1,000 types of minerals, it is difficult to process them because energy sources must be imported at great expense. *6-Kuznetsk:* Russia's important manufacturing center situated east of the Urals which possesses much coal and iron ore. *7-Silesia:* The leading manufacturing center outside of Russia in Eastern Europe.

Japan (441-442): Other than a large, disciplined population, Japan has few good geographic assets. However, after World War II, it produced large quantities of cheap goods, due to its inexpensive labor force. Japan's economic planners foresaw more competition in low-end consumer goods, so it changed its industrial base to higher-end electronic goods and precision instruments made by a more educated work-force. Today, Japan leads the world in the export of consumer goods. In Japan, industry is concentrated in the central region between Tokyo and Nagasaki.

Situational Factors for Factory Location (442): Transporting inputs of a product to a factory and the finished product to the consumer are the factors that influence the situation of an industrial facility. An optimal location will provide the low costs of transportation to a firm. A company will tend to either locate its factory near the greatest source of its inputs or near its consumer base, whichever is more profitable.

Copper Industry (442-443): Copper ore in North America is low-grade, with most of it being less than one percent copper. The result is a very heavy ore which is expensive to transport. Copper concentration is a **bulk-reducing industry** which refines the ore, removing 98 percent of the impurities. Proximity to copper mines determines the locations of copper smelters, refineries, and mills because high transportation costs would make other alternatives not profitable. The only major exception is Baltimore; it imports its copper from foreign countries into its port.

Steel Industry (443-444): Steel-making is another bulk-reducing industry. In the mid-1800's steel making was concentrated in **southwestern Pennsylvania** around Pittsburgh because both of its inputs, coal and iron ore, were mined there. However, the discovery of high-grade ore in the **Mesabi Range of northern Minnesota** near Lake Superior, as well as technology that decreased the proportion of coal in the manufacturing process, shifted steel-making to many cities on the shores of the other Great Lakes, such as Toledo, Cleveland, Chicago, and Gary. The Great Lakes provide very cheap transportation for the bulky iron ore and coal. Minimills are an emerging player in the steel-making industry; proximity to market determines successful mills today, as well as the fact that scrap metal derived from that same market is available.

Bulk-Gaining Industries (444-446): Bulk-gaining industries produce a commodity that gains weight and/or volume during the production process, which affect transportation costs. For example, the soft drink industry uses cans and bottles, syrup, and water. Syrup is concentrated and easy to transport, empty bottles and cans are relatively light, and water is found in any population center. Consequently, companies tend to locate their industries in local markets to reduce transportation costs of the final product. Beer bottlers also tend to follow a similar pattern of locating several facilities around the country, thus minimizing the cost of transportation to the consumer. More commonly, bulk-gaining products gain more volume than weight. When the sum of all the parts of a product, such as a car, surpass the individual components in weight, it becomes critical to locate assembly plants near the consumer market (See Box 10-1).

Perishable Products (446-447): Food products such as bread and milk have a limited shelf life, so it is imperative to supply them to consumers as quickly as possible. Such food products are processed near the consumer market. However, other goods that are frozen, canned, or otherwise long-lasting may be manufactured in a place remote from consumers. Newspapers are a perishable product, because they are only valuable when their information is current. Accordingly, many newspaper publishers in the U.S. publish papers in the same areas that dually act as distribution centers to reduce transportation costs. Still, with the innovations in satellite technology, the New York Times, Wall Street Journal, and U.S.A Today can electronically transmit their papers contents to regional publishers without having to physically move the copy.

Single Market Manufacturers (447-448): Single market manufacturers make products that are sold in one market. For example, several times a year, buyers from individual clothing stores come to New York from all over the world to order clothing that they will retail in department stores in the coming fashion season. Therefore, high-style clothing makers tend to cluster around New York.

Ship, Rail, Truck, or Air Transportation (448): These are the four primary modes of freight transportation. In general, the farther the distance traveled, the cheaper per kilometer cost. The costs per kilometer differ in part because of different loading and unloading costs. For short distances, trucks are most frequently used; trains have an advantage for somewhat longer distances. Extremely long distances are best accomplished by ship transport for it is cheap over such lengthy ranges. Air transport is expensive, but it very quick and is used when time efficiency is a must, as with perishable and time-sensitive goods.

Break-of-Bulk Points (448-449): Break-of-bulk points are places where transfer among transportation modes is possible. For example, a steel mill near Baltimore may receive coal via rail from Appalachia and South American iron ore by a ship in its port. Furthermore, costs rise each time goods are transferred from one mode of transportation to another due to loading/unloading costs. Though situational factors remain important, their relative importance has declined over time due to increasing importance of *site factors*.

Site Factors (449-452): Costs that directly influence business can be divided into *land, labor,* and *capital. Land* is an important factor because it varies much in cost, potential for expansion, proximity to energy, and amenities. Generally, modern factories tend to be located in rural or suburban areas, where large tracts of land may be obtained substantially cheaper than land in the central part of a city. The ability to add more buildings in the future is also a consideration for obtaining real estate in these areas. In the past, factories were located near rivers and forests because energy was ordinarily gained from those sources. Today, electricity has replaced wood and running water as an energy source, so it is a important variable in factory location. It should be noted that hydro-electricity from running water is a cheap source of electricity today. Some businesses locate in places like the American Southwest because of climate, sports franchises, topography and other amenities that are to their liking. In industries that are *labor-intensive*, where *labor* is a large input in the manufacturing process, location is of keen importance. At the beginning of this chapter, maquiladoras were mentioned as alternative sites for companies formerly located in the U.S. due to the cheap labor found in Mexico. Generally, the industries that have relocated in Mexico are labor-intensive. In order to initially set up a factory or plant in a given place, *capital* needs to be secured for financing of the venture. In LDC's where monies cannot be secured, industrialization is stalled, thus allowing the country to remain less developed than other countries. Unstable political systems, high debt levels, and ill-perceived economic policies retard the flow of investment into LDC's.

Textile and Clothing Industries (452-456): Textile industries generally require less skilled, low-cost labor. There are three steps in textile production: *1-Spinning fibers* to make yarn, *2-Weaving* or *knitting* yarn into fabric, and *3-Cutting* and *sewing* the fabric into clothing or other products. The natural fiber cotton is processed where it is grown. The U.S., China, India, Pakistan, and Uzbekistan grow over half of the world's cotton and process an equal proportion of the world's cotton fiber. Unlike cotton, wool is not processed in the same areas where it is grown. Weaving cotton fabric is mostly carried out in LDC's because of the high labor input involved. Most cotton clothing in the world is produced in MDC's in Europe and North America, though in recent years production has tended to shift to LDC's. In the U.S. textile companies have moved locations to take advantage of the lowest paid workers they can use. For example, during most of the 1800's textile and clothing firms were located in the Northeast because large supplies of European immigrants would toil long hours in harsh *sweatshops* for little pay. Enough time and frustration passed so that the workers eventually organized and demanded better pay and benefits. At this time the firms sought out workers in the Southeast who demanded less pay for longer hours due to a generally depressed economy. Since the clothing industry was actually a step-up from the previous occupations of many of the workers, they were less-inclined to promote union participation.

Skilled Labor Industry (456-458): Like Japan in the past, the U.S. is finding that higher skilled jobs which better compensate workers are more lucrative in today's competitive global economy. In the past, workers were traditionally assigned a single job, a single responsibility. Geographers dub this practice *Fordist*, after Henry Ford, who developed modern factory management techniques early in this century. However, today many workers are assigned to teams that carry out a series of tasks. This new, innovative approach is called *post-Fordist*.

Obstacles to Optimum Location (458): Many industries have become footloose, meaning that many places can accommodate them without any major negative impacts upon their costs in transportation, land, labor, and capital. Proficiency in identifying the best of all potential sites varies widely, thus one executive in charge of such a task may actually find the best possible site, another less-competent executive unaware of modern technologies such as Geographic Information Systems (GIS), may just find an acceptable site. Since locational searches are somewhat expensive, demand and time constraints force some companies to make less-than-perfect locational decisions.

Stagnant Demand for Goods (458-459): During most of the last two centuries more people are constantly being added to the world's consumer market. As more factories were opened throughout the world, more of their employees gained disposable income. However, by the 1970's demand had slowed considerably in MDC's, mainly because of market saturation and stabilized population growth rates. Also, consumers have matured, requiring quality goods that are replaced less frequently than in the past. Technology decreased the relative importance of steel, while plastics and other substitutes have replaced steel.

Increased Capacity Worldwide in Steel (459-461): While demand has stagnated for products such as steel since the mid-1970's, the efficiency of the global economy to produce them has increased, thus reducing the number of facilities to produce such goods and, consequently, bringing some unemployment to certain economic sectors. For example, during most of the 1800's, the United Kingdom out-produced the rest of the world in industrial goods. However, as more countries entered competition with Britain for market share of industry, Britain's world domination was reduced. Today, the world has many industrial bases in many parts of the world. LDC's have also had a similar effect upon MDC's; as LDC's have enlarged their industrial bases, MDC industrial share has shrunken. LDC's such as India, Brazil, South Korea, and China have increased their steel production while MDC's have decreased their production.

Trading Blocs (461-463): As different countries in the world face increasing competition brought about by technology and cheaper transportation throughout the world, three regional blocs of countries have formed alliances to ensure exports and to insulate themselves from competition. These three are the **Western Hemisphere, Western Europe,** and **East Asia.** For example, the **North American Free Trade Agreement, NAFTA,** was implemented in 1994 and will eventually negate all tariffs on goods traded between member countries, which currently include the U.S., Canada, and Mexico. If a country belongs to a bloc it can theoretically export goods to bloc members without tariff-penalties. As well, it must be willing to import goods from member countries without adding import tariffs. In such an environment, comparative advantages may be realized, ushering forth more productive economies. Although internal cooperation exists within trade blocs, each bloc strives to decrease effective efforts in trade from competing blocs. Consequently, it is common for a member of an East Asian bloc (such as Japan) to restrict imports on goods being sold by a member of NAFTA (such as the U.S.).

Transnational Corporations (463): Also known as **multinational corporations**, these firms have parts of their operations located in a number of different countries which, ideally, reflect the comparative advantage yielded by each country. Historically, the U.S. dominated this type of company, but Japan, Germany, France, and the United Kingdom have recently entered this realm of capitalism. For example, some firms have located labor-intensive industries in Mexico because, due to existing low wages and proximity to the U.S. market, Mexico is more profitable as a factory site than most places. Japanese auto companies, using the same philosophy, have located some factories in the U.S. because labor is cheaper than in Japan.

Variation in Western Europe and the U.S. (463-465): Industry and wealth are not spread evenly across the world nor across trading blocs. For example, in France, areas near Paris have large concentrations of wealth and industry while the south and west suffer poorer economic realities. The northern part of Italy has three times the per capita income of the southern reaches of the peninsula and Sicily. In order to develop under-developed parts of the European Community grants, tax reductions, and other forms of government aid are often furnished as incentives to invest in less-prosperous areas. In the U.S. the historically poor South has witnessed much economic growth due to government policy and evolving site preferences. The formerly solid core of industry in the U.S. has experienced little or no economic growth in recent decades.

LDC Industrial Problems (465): If LDC's are to mature economically into MDC's then they must develop their economies in similar ways. Even so, obstacles hinder this evolution. Most LDC's in Latin America, Africa, and Asia are far from the wealthy markets of the trading blocs. Due to their geographic remoteness, LDC's must invest scarce resources in transportation that could otherwise be invested in education, infrastructure, or national strategic (long term) planning. *Infrastructures* include universities, communications, roads, and utilities. LDC's still face the high cost of initially installing the expensive amenities that facilitate industrial growth.

Two Traits for LDC Industrial Growth (465-466): Economic geographers have named two phenomena indispensable for industrial growth; raw material access and favorable site factors: A country will more likely be developed if it has good access to coal, oil, iron, and other raw materials that can be used as an industrial input. Favorable site factors include cheap, plentiful labor. During the twentieth century, multinational companies have selected places to locate factories, using labor as a weighted variable. Consequently, places with inexpensive labor have attracted the firms wanting to locate factories.

Case Study; NAFTA (467-468): In order to better compete in the global economy the North American Free Trade Agreement was created by the U.S., Canada, and Mexico. The accord would eliminate tariffs between the countries, thus encouraging trade to occur. Many Americans believe jobs will be promptly exported to Mexico due to the lower wages existing there. Skeptics believe that workers will be exploited and the environment will be damaged because of *laissez-faire* practices in Mexico.

CLOSING REMARKS

The industrial revolution began in Britain around 1750 due to a series of innovations in technology, and has since diffused throughout many parts of the rest of the world. Yet, many countries yearn to become more fully integrated into it. Still, most of Earth's industrial output remains in the most intensely industrialized parts of Europe, Asia, and

North America. In today's world, firms are better served if they find territory whose inhabitants work efficiently and cheaply. Nevertheless, in today's world of declining demand due to market saturation and other factors, it is ever more difficult to fill orders.

KEY TERMS AND CONCEPTS

Maquiladoras: Factories built by U.S. companies in Mexico near the U.S. border, to take advantage of much lower labor costs in Mexico. New maquiladoras are often located outside of the border area due to incentives given by local governments.

Cottage Industry: Manufacturing based in homes rather than in a factory, commonly found before the Industrial Revolution. An important cottage industry was textile manufacturing.

Steam Engine: An efficient engine patented by James Watt, a Scot from Glasgow, in 1769. It was the most important single development in increasing capacity and profitability of factories during the Industrial Revolution.

Blast Furnace: A furnace that is blasted with air, thus made extremely hot for the smelting of iron. In blast furnaces iron is cast into "pig" castings to be later remolded in the form of products.

Railway System: The locomotives and iron rails upon which they are operated. The invention of the locomotive symbolized the impact of engineering on the industrial revolution.

Textiles: A fabric made by weaving, used in making clothes. In the U.S. the textile base has shifted from the Northeast to the Southeast due to cheaper, more cooperative (less unionized) work forces.

Synthetic Fibers: Natural fibers that are combined with chemicals. Today, the largest textile companies are owned by chemical companies.

Canning: A method of preserving food in glass bottles that had been sterilized in boiling water. The invention of the more versatile, cheaper tin can made this process expand.

Right-to-work state: A U.S. state that has a law preventing the negotiation of a contract that requires workers to join a union as a condition of employment. They are prevalent in the Southeast.

Situational Factors: Location factors related to the transportation of materials into and away from a factory. For example, a copper smelter would likely be located close to a copper mine where the ore could be bought inexpensively to the smelter, and the refined material transported inexpensively to plants for further processing.

Site Factors: Location factors related to the costs of factors of production inside the plant, such as land, labor, and capital. For example, the site characteristics of a maquiladora tend to be dominated by cheap labor.

Bulk-reducing Industry: An industry in which the final product weighs less or comprises a lower volume than the inputs. The refinement of petroleum or steel is such an industry.

Bulk-gaining Industries: An industry in which the final product weighs more or comprises a greater volume than the inputs. The manufacture of automobiles is an example of this industry.

Perishable Products: An industry for which rapid delivery of the product to consumers is a critical factor. Food and newspapers (which become value-less as time goes by) are examples.

Break-of-bulk Point: A location where transfer is necessary from one mode of transportation to another. Airports and seaports are examples; they make excellent locations for distribution centers.

Labor-intensive Industry: An industry for which labor costs comprise a high percentage of total expenses. Low-skilled, labor-intensive industries are often exported from MDC's to LDC's.

Fordist: Form of mass production in which each worker is assigned one specific task to perform repeatedly. It is named after automobile mogul Henry Ford.

Post-Fordist: Teams of workers that perform a variety of tasks. This philosophy has become popular in the U.S. in recent years.

Trading Blocs: Regional economic affiliations which increase trade between member countries by reducing tariffs between them. Three major blocks are in the Western Hemisphere, Western Europe, and East Asia.

North American Free Trade Agreement (NAFTA): The regional trading bloc which includes the U.S., Canada, and Mexico. Other countries of the Western Hemisphere are likely to join, Costa Rica and Chile being among the next countries to join NAFTA.

Transnational Corporations: Firms which operate different parts of their companies in different locations around the globe.

New International Division of Labor: Transfer of some types of jobs, especially those requiring low-paid less skilled workers, from relatively developed to developing countries. Many people believe that freer trade will lead to an exodus of low-skilled jobs to LDC's where labor is cheaper.

1. _____ are plants located in Mexico due to the cheap labor found there.

Maquiladoras

2. The Industrial Revolution began in the _____ _____ around 1750.

United Kingdom

3. The root of the Industrial Revolution was _____ brought about by innovative ideas.

technology

4. In 1769 James Watt invented the _____ _____, which greatly increased the capacity of factories.

steam engine

5. Before the Industrial Revolution manufacturing was often farmed out to people's homes in the form of the _____ _____.

cottage industry

6. In order to process iron into steel, _____ replaced charcoal for heating the iron.

coal

7. Due to the interdependence of coal and iron, steel mills tended to be located near _____ fields.

coal

8. _____ _____ and Matthew Boulton established the Soho Foundry in Birmingham, England in 1795.

James Watt

9. The invention of the _____, or "iron horse," superseded the canal as a mode of transportation.

railway

10. _____, or woven fabric, were tremendously affected by the Industrial Revolution.

Textiles

11. _____ acid was used to bleach cotton fabric.

Sulfuric

12. Nicholas Appert of France developed _____ in 1810 to prolong the shelf-life of various food products.

canning

13. The _____ _____ of the 1851 World's Fair symbolized the Industrial Revolution to that point.

Crystal Palace

14. The continents of _____ and _____ _____ were the first and second to benefit from the industrial revolution.

Europe, North America

15. Ironically, the infrastructures of _____ and _____ were rebuilt with aid from the U.S. after World War II, allowing them to more fully develop afterward.

Germany, Japan

16. The first textile mill in the U.S. was built in 1791 in Pawtucket, Rhode Island by _____ _____.

Samuel Slater

17. When natural fibers and chemicals are combined, _____ fibers result.

synthetic

18. Today, the largest textile companies in the world are owned by _____ companies.

chemical

19. Industry in North America is concentrated in _____ Canada and _____ U.S..

southeastern, northeastern

20. _____ are known as right-to-work states.

Southeastern

21. Right-to-work states do not permit the mandatory membership in _____.

unions

22. The Rhine-Ruhr Valley is the most important industrial area in Western _____.

Europe

23. Throughout the twentieth century, _____ _____ has lost market share due to increases in global competition.

Great Britain

24. Most of _____ industries and population are concentrated in the Po River valley, in the northern reaches of the country.

Italy's

25. Over 1,000 minerals are found in the _____ mountains of Russia.

Ural

26. _____ has few natural resources and is far-removed from the markets of North America and Europe, but is a powerful industrial power.

Japan

27. Variables involving the transportation of materials to and from a factory are called _____ factors.

situational

28. Unique characteristics of a location contribute to its _____ factors.

site

29. The steel industry is a bulk-_____ industry.

reducing

30. The _____ Range of Minnesota supplies high grade iron ore to the steel mills situated along the shores of the Great Lakes.　　Mesabi

31. Fresh food and newspapers are known as _____ products because they quickly lose value with age.　　perishable

32. _____ is the most expensive mode of transportation for all distances.　　Air

33. Ships are the cheapest mode of transportation over _____ distances.　　long

34. Many modern factories have shifted to _____ or _____ areas.　　suburban, rural

35. A _____-_____ industry is one in which the cost of labor makes up a high percentage of the total cost.　　labor-intensive

36. Local and national governments attempt to lure industry within their boundaries by offering financial _____.　　incentives

37. The management philosophy whereby one worker performs a single task is called _____.　　Fordist

38. Regional economic differences within are known as _____.　　disparities

CHAPTER ELEVEN

SETTLEMENTS

OVERVIEW

People are not uniformly dispersed across the landscape. Some people prefer to live in comparatively isolated areas while others prefer to live near other humans in settlements. Settlements are further divided into a number of sub-groupings because of diverse locations, sizes, and shapes. Chapter Eleven describes the variety of settlements that have developed in the world, and gives reasons for such development.

SELECTED NOTES

Obtaining Goods In Romania (475): The country of Romania in Eastern Europe depends on public transportation to carry its citizens to their destinations, instead of relying primarily on private transportation. Its largest city, Bucharest, has two million people. There are few cities with populations between 1,000 and 10,000 to provide local services. There are no cities with populations between 350,000 and two million people to provide regional services. The Romanian people must travel long distances to find basic services. Trips that would take a few minutes by car often end up taking hours using public transportation.

Settlements for Cultural Reasons (475-476): Today settlements grow for economic reasons. Historically, however, they were established for cultural reasons. The first permanent settlements were located near burial sites, where *churches* and places of worship were eventually constructed. People settled to *shelter families* while males were on long excursions in search of food. Some places were settled for defense from invaders. *Walls* were built around urban areas for thousands of years, until gunpowder and cannon nullified their effectiveness in the 1800's.

Settlements for Economic Reasons (476-477): At some point in history humans observed that by storing food for times of need, they could survive better. Many early settlements were formed around a *warehousing center*. When farming became a prominent occupation, communities were formed around *agricultural centers*. As artisans and skilled-labor became increasingly important as time passed cities also became a hub for large numbers of these professionals as *manufacturing centers*. Some settlements were at the cross roads between cities of different talents and the trade that developed established them as *trade centers*. At trade centers people came from outlying areas to barter their goods for unavailable items.

Rural Settlements (477-481): Today, more people live in rural areas than in urban areas. When people reside in a clustered *village* or *hamlet*, they often work in surrounding fields. Often the inhabitants of these settlements will be responsible for farming a few pieces of land, which may be held by an individual or a landowner who dictates farm activity. *Circular rural settlements* are used in Africa by the Masai and southern Africans to protect their cattle in the kraal (corral) in the center of the settlement. Germans used circular settlement patterns as a way of organizing homes and economic activities such as agriculture. *Linear settlements* form landscape patterns in places inhabited by French peoples. In places like Quebec, Canada property would extend back from lines of communication and transportation (rivers, roads, and dikes) for long distances creating *long lots*. Farmers living in isolated farms instead of villages create patterns of *dispersed rural settlements*. Unfortunately, this meant that many farmers, after centuries of land inheritance, owned very fragmented pieces of land. Between 1750 and 1850 the British government began the *enclosure movement* which consolidated many of the fragmented farms in Britain. Consequently, many people moved to cities in England to become employed by the engines of the industrial revolution.

Settlements in Colonial America (481-482): People who came to *New England* from England settled in villages like those from the homelands. People lived in a *clustered settlement*, built around a public space called the commons. Land was awarded to church members in one to five acre plots. When populations grew, new settlers were forced to move West to find land uninhabited by Europeans. As time wore on, the influence of religion declined along with the importance of clustered settlements. In the *Southeast*, small farms first appeared in the 1600's but were soon replaced by plantations. Plantations were large farms that used cheap labor (slaves or indentured servants) and grew cash crops such as tobacco and cotton. Services needed by the plantation (the blacksmith, bakery, kitchen, and housing) were clustered around the mansion. In the *Middle Atlantic,* Europeans from Germany, Holland, Britain, Ireland, Scotland and Sweden settled. They farmed and supplied most of the pioneers for the American West where they continued to practice agriculture.

Urban Settlements (483-487): Although most of the planet's people reside in rural areas, the percentage of people living in urban areas is rapidly increasing because of a perceived better life. One of the oldest cities on Earth is *Ur*, located in modern day Iraq. The city contained a temple known as a *ziggurat*, 250 acres, and was encircled by a wall. Other ancient settlements were in China, Egypt, and the Indus Valley. Early settlements in Europe were Troy in Asia Minor and Knosses, Crete. They were organized into city-states, which were urban areas, and their surrounding countrysides. The number of cities in Europe grew rapidly in the 7th and 8th centuries B.C. in Italy, Sicily, and Spain. One of the first dominating ancient cities in ancient Europe was *Athens*, Greece. The rise of the Roman empire encouraged urban settlement to help manage the territory. *Rome*, its administrative, cultural, and commercial center was integral to the empire's success. In the eleventh century new settlements began to appear in Europe. Feudal lords allowed their serfs to move to cities in exchange for periodic military service. The typical

European city was compact, dense and surrounded by a wall. Palaces, churches, and public buildings were arranged in the center of town. Until the onset of the Industrial Revolution the five most important cities in the world were in Asia: Baghdad, Constantinople, Kyoto, Changan, and Hangchow (both in China).

The Urban Explosion (487-490): Rome, the largest city in ancient times, probably had no more people than Des Moine, Iowa. Today, more than 100 cities in the world contain more than two million people. During the last 200 years people have increasingly migrated to urban areas; cities have experienced more natural increase causing *urbanization*. In 1800, only three percent of the world's population was urban; today forty percent of the population is urban. By 1900, nine of the world's ten largest cities were in the U.S. and Europe. MDC's tend to have higher proportions of their populations in cities than LDC's. Most MDC's have manufacturing and service centers which employ people in urban settings while LDC's are dominated by rural agricultural workers. The largest city in 1992, as classified by the U.S. Census Bureau, was the *Tokyo-Yokohama* region in Japan. Second was Mexico City. Urban areas in less developed countries are attracting large numbers of rural people because, although their economic opportunities are not great, they are still better than the economically desolate countryside.

Social Differences Between Urban and Rural Settlements (490-491): Urban and rural areas have very different "personalities". Urban areas are very large, allowing one to personally know few people relative to the overall population, whereas in rural areas people often know very high percentages of the populations. Higher population densities in cities make people more competitive for virtually everything from living space to jobs. In large, urban centers there is a greater variety of people, so there are more lifestyle choices. Deviations in eligion, sexuality, or personal appearance are more tolerated in large cities. Even so, people in cities can also feel lonely because of their environment's impersonal nature.

Problems in Defining Urban Settings (491-493): A *city* is a urban settlement which has been formally incorporated into an independent, self-governing unit. A city can collect taxes, elect officials, and must provide essential services. Cities are not given any rights in the U.S. Constitution, as are counties and states. Until recently, cities could expand their sphere of influence through *annexation*, the addition of new land to within city boundaries. In the 1800's many people desired annexation because that meant better services than were previously provided. Today, high taxes and less authority over large bureaucratic government encourage many people to remain independent of large urban areas. Within the U.S. there are *20,000* different local governments. Often their boundaries lie along obscure routes, creating an atmosphere of confusion when local services respond. The *urbanized area* is the largest city in an area, its *central city*, as well as the built-up, surrounding suburbs. Unfortunately, statistics are not kept on urbanized areas. Still, the influence of a city can be measured far beyond its legal limits, for many people the city is the economic and cultural base.

Metropolitan Statistical Area (493-494, 495): The U.S. Census Bureau has created the *metropolitan statistical area (MSA)*. An MSA is a city of 50,000 residents, its county, and all surrounding counties whose residents are densely populated and work in non-farm jobs, and which had a population growth rate of at least 20 percent during the 1970's. Ten percent of the population of adjacent counties must live in urbanized areas. MSA's often overlap and include much non-urban land. If MSA's are adjacent and overlap commuting patterns, they may be combined into *consolidated metropolitan statistical areas (CMSA's)*. It is important to many counties to be designated as MSA's and CMSA's because the federal government doles out money to places of that level. Exposure due to statistical data at that level is also an important factor in attracting economic investment by business.

Megalopolis (494-495): A long, continuous urban complex which combines several MSA's is often called a *megalopolis*, coined by geographer Jean Gottman. The long stretch of urbanization between Boston and Washington, DC is a megalopolis. Boundaries between metropolitan areas of the megalopolis overlap and do not have significantly large, continuous rural areas separating them.

Metropolitan Government (495-496): Due to the enormous number of governments in the U.S., it is very difficult to coordinate them in a team effort to solve regional problems such as traffic, solid-waste disposal, and affordable housing. *Metropolitan* areas in the U.S. are commonly managed by a council of government that is authorized to perform overall planning of the area which local governments cannot do. *Federation governments*, such as the one ruling Toronto's area, divide duties of government between two tiers: one regional and several local component governments. *Consolidated governments* are formed when cities and their respective counties combine governments. In the United Kingdom the federal government has the power to redefine the boundaries of local governments. In the 1980s' the UK redefined many of its cities' borders.

Service Concentrations in Urban Areas (496-497): A *service* is any activity that fulfills a human want or need and returns money to those who provide it. *Tertiary sectors* diffuse and distribute services. *Quaternary* sectors provide banking, legal services, and retailing to other service businesses, though not to individuals. *Quinary sectors* provide services for the well-being and personal improvement of individual consumers. In the U.S., employment has declined in the primary and secondary sectors but has increased in the service industries. The number and presence of some retail services such as McDonalds give geographers information about the urban level to which different cities belong.

Factors in Locating a Service (497-500): When a company desires to locate a branch of its operations in a certain market, the location of the prospective business must have *access to markets*. The area surrounding a service from which customers are found is the *market area* or *hinterland* of a business. Market areas are examples of *nodal regions*, which are illustrated by drawing a circle on a map with the vertex representing the location of the business being analyzed. The *range* of a market is the maximum distance people are willing to travel to use that business. If there are competing businesses in the range, then the location of the business needs to be modified so that a good threshold of customers will be present. The ***threshold*** is the minimum number of people needed to support the service of a firm. These people produce revenue, which makes the firm profitable. By using Census data, computer software, and performing marketing research a firm may ascertain these figures.

Selecting a Location for a Service (500-501): Once an acceptable threshold and range has been found, the precise location of a firm should be established. Geographers use the ***gravity model*** to locate businesses in areas of best potential. In a linear settlement, the best location for a business is the geographic midpoint between the extreme corners of population.

Central Place Theory (501-506): The market center to which people come for the exchange of goods and services is called the ***central place***. The central place is located so that it maximizes accessibility by the people living in its dominion., Conceived by ***Walter Christaller*** and further refined by August Losch and Brian Berry, ***Central Place Theory*** is the geographical concept which explains the significance of central places. Although circles can be drawn to represent the markets of various firms, six-sided ***hexagons*** are preferred for they fit easily together and tend to be less confusing. Four hierarchies of hexagons represent, in ascending order: hamlets, villages, towns, and cities, shown in Figure 11-6. The size of the hexagon is determined by its market. Within cities divisions can also be made to determine internal market for businesses such as grocery stores and gasoline stations. The ***rank-size rule*** is applicable when a country's Nth largest city contains 1/N of the population of the largest settlement. The ***primate city*** exists when the largest city in the country possesses over twice the population of the next largest city. LDC's tend to have primate cities more often than MDC's.

Economic Base of Settlements (506-507): Cities often specialize their industrial base in specific ways. For example, Washington, DC is mainly government-oriented while Las Vegas focuses on entertainment. ***Basic industries*** sell their goods and services outside of their community and ***non-basic industries*** sell their goods and services mainly to people within their community. Basic industries are very important because they inject money into the local economy, allowing non-basic industries to develop which directly serve the populace. A community's unique collection of economic industries define its economic base. Different regions in the U.S. tend to have certain industrial types for economic base. For example, the Southeast is more likely to have textile industries as their base than are other areas in the U.S..

Economic Restructuring and the Urban System (507-508): Basic industries used to be mainly manufacturing but have increasingly been replaced by service industries. Pittsburgh was once supported by the steel industry but time has made medical industries the strongest segment of its economic base today. Cities have often structured themselves around unique economic bases. The San Jose and Boston areas specialize in computing and data processing industries while cities like Austin and Orlando distinguish themselves with high-technology industries.

<u>Types of Cities (508-509)</u>: Geographers enumerate four different levels of cities based on roles in global services: world cities, regional command and control centers, specialized producer-service centers, and dependent centers. London, New York, and Tokyo are in the first class of world cities. A second tier includes Chicago, Washington, Los Angeles, Brussels, Frankfurt, and Paris. These cities include regional and command centers and also act as the headquarters for many large corporations. Third tier cities specialize in producer-service centers with highly specialized services. Dependent city centers are the fourth tier cities which provide relatively unskilled labor.

CLOSING REMARKS

Settlements were originally established for non-economic reasons. The importance of a solid economic base for settlements has become very important, especially after the Industrial Revolution. Due to changing technology, economic success is more often found in urban settlements. Consequently, the world's population has steadily been migrating to cities during the last two-hundred years. Cities are not only attractive because of lucrative jobs, but also because of the many services and goods provided.

KEY TERMS AND CONCEPTS

Settlement: A permanent collection of buildings and inhabitants. Cities are born from settlements.

Rural Settlement: A settlement in which the principal occupation of the residents is agriculture. Rural settlements are very common in less developed countries.

Urban Settlements: A settlement in which the principle economic activities are manufacturing, warehousing, trading, and provision of services.

Clustered Rural Settlement: A rural settlement in which the houses and farm buildings of each family are situated close to each other and fields surround the settlement. Farming villages are classified as this type of settlement.

Dispersed Rural Settlements: A rural settlement pattern characterized by isolated farms rather than clustered villages.

Enclosure Movement: The process of consolidating small land holdings into a smaller number of larger farms in England during the eighteenth century. The English farms were made more efficient by the changes.

Plantation: A large farm that used many workers to produce tobacco and cotton for sale in Europe and the northern colonies. Plantations became ineffective in the U.S. after the Emancipation Proclamation of 1863.

City-state: An independent state comprised of a city and the surrounding countryside. San Marino and the Vatican are contemporary examples.

Urbanization: The increase in the number of urban dwellers as well as the increase in the overall percentage of urban dwellers. It has increased by a large margin in the last two hundred years.

Annexation: Adding land area legally to a city. Many people in the U.S. resist annexation because it usually brings higher taxes.

Central City: The core of a large, urbanized area. Los Angeles is the core of a large urbanized area which contains many other cities.

Metropolitan Statistical Area (MSA): In the United States, a central city with at least 50,000 people, the country within which the city is located, and adjacent counties meeting one of several criteria indicating a functional connection to the central city.

Megalopolis: Continuous, adjacent MSA's which form a massive urban complex, such as the urban corridor between Boston and Washington.

Consolidated Metropolitan Statistical Area (CMSA): Two or more adjacent MSA's with overlapping commuting patterns.

Council of Government: A cooperative agency consisting of representatives of local governments in a metropolitan area in the United States. Planning powers are often held by councils.

Service: Any activity that fulfills a human want or need and returns money to those who provide it. In recent years this economic sector has grown faster than any other.

Market Area (Hinterland): The area surrounding a central place, from which people are attracted to use the place's goods and services. Its size determines the number of businesses which may exist in the area's core.

Range: The maximum distance people are willing to travel to use a service. The less common the service, generally, the longer people will travel to use it.

Threshold: The minimum number of people needed to support the service. Due to high population densities, thresholds are more easily found in urban areas than in rural areas.

Gravity Model: A model that holds that the potential use of a good or service at a particular location is directly related to the number of people in a location and inversely related to the distance people must travel to reach the good or service.

Central Place: A market center for the exchange of goods and services by people attracted from the surrounding area.

Central Place Theory: A theory that explains the distribution of settlements based on the fact that settlements serve as market centers for people living in the surrounding area. Larger settlements are fewer and farther apart than smaller settlements and serve a large population base.

Rank-size Rule: A pattern of settlements in a country, where the Nth largest settlement is 1/N the population of the largest settlement. Countries where this rule holds true tend to be more developed.

Primate City: The largest settlement in a country if it has more than twice as many inhabitants as the second-ranking settlement. Paris, France is an example.

Basic Industries: Industries that sell their products primarily to consumers outside the settlement. These businesses inject fresh currency into the local economy.

Nonbasic Industries: Industries that sell their products primarily to consumers in the community. A large number and variety indicate a high standard of living for the populace.

Economic Base: A community's collection of basic industries. Often cities have created a special niche as an economic base.

CHAPTER ELEVEN

1. The primate city of Romania is _____.   Bucharest

2. A permanent collection of buildings and inhabitants in which
people live is a _____.   settlement

3. Religious settlements began around _____ grounds.   burial

4. In prehistoric times, men were responsible for _____, while   hunting
women were in charge of _____ as a means for survival.   gathering

5. Places where groups met to barter goods that were not widely
available were called _____ _____.   trading centers

6. _____ is the main economic activity in rural settlements.   Agriculture

7. A clustered rural settlement is commonly known as a _____ or   village,
_____.   hamlet

8. _____ villages in southern Africa have enclosures for livestock.   Kraal

9. The _____-_____ is a pattern of settlement common to the   long-lot
French settled areas in North America.

10. The _____ movement brought greater agricultural efficiency   enclosure
to Britain, but destroyed the self-contained village way of life.

11. The public centers of New England villages are often called
the _____.   commons

12. In New England, land was _____ to church members rather   awarded
than sold.

13. Large farms in the Southeast called _____ produced cash   plantations
crops such as _____ and _____.   cotton, tobacco

14. Along with slaves, _____ _____ often worked on plantations   indentured servants
for a few years after they arrived in the Americas.

15. People who settled the U.S. frontier most often came from
_____ _____ rural settlements.   Middle, Atlantic

16. The percentage of _____ settlements has been steadily increasing for 200 years.   urban

17. Most people on Earth live in _____ settlements.   rural

18. One of the oldest settled cities is _____ in Mesopotamia.   Ur

19. Knossos and Troy were early _____-_____ in the Mediterranean.   city-states

20. _____ was probably the first city in the ancient world to reach 100,000 people.   Athens

21. The fall of the _____ Empire saw a decline in urban settlements in their realm of influence.   Roman

22. Prior to the Industrial Revolution, the world's five largest cities were found on the continent of _____.   Asia

23. In the early 1800's, _____ exceeded two million in population.   London

24. According to the U.S. Census Bureau, the largest urban area in the world was found in the country of _____.   Japan

25. A larger variety of cultures and lifestyles are found in _____ areas than in rural areas.   urban

26. All U.S. states are divided into counties except the state of _____.   Louisiana

27. Cities legally add territory to their area through the process of _____.   addition annexation

28. Most U.S. metropolitan areas have a _____ form of government, which includes representatives from many different local governments.   council

29. A _____ area is the surrounding domain from which customers are attracted.   market

30. The farthest distance one is willing to travel to purchase a good is its _____.   range

31. A _____ _____ is a market center for the exchange of goods and services for an area.

central place

32. Central place theory was developed by the German, _____ _____.

Walter Christaller

33. A city which is over twice as large as the next largest city in a country is a _____ _____.

primate city

34. _____ _____ are industries which sell products primarily outside of their community.

Basic industries

35. A community's unique collection of basic industries comprise its _____ _____.

economic base

36. The three most dominant cities in the world are _____, _____, and _____.

London, New York Tokyo

CHAPTER TWELVE

URBAN PATTERNS

OVERVIEW

The core of a city has traditionally been its downtown. Religious centers, government, businesses and public spaces are often found there. Chapter Twelve describes different characteristics of urban centers and their peripheries found in different places in the world. People tend to live near other people who share similar geo-demographic traits. This chapter also describes the different living arrangements between poor and rich people in urban areas.

SELECTED NOTES

Social Differences Between Inner Cities and Suburbs (520): Many people in the inner city have low incomes and many children. Since education is not attained by a high percentage of inner city people, hope for better jobs and incomes is dismal. Many services and stores have migrated to the suburbs because they cannot be used by people from the inner cities. Only a few miles from inner cities are suburbs where more affluent people live, the children attend better schools, and receive a better education. However, since housing and taxes are more expensive in the suburbs, it is difficult or impossible for inner city people to migrate to the more favorable suburbs.

Services of the CBD (521-523): In cities, most economic activities occur in its center or the downtown. This area is called the *central business district* or *CBD*. There are three types of retail stores in a CBD. *1-Shops with high thresholds* are business-like department stores which need a large number of customers to support them. Due to competition from the suburbs, the number of these stores in CBD's has declined. *2-Shops with high ranges* tend to be stores that are very specialized and not found in many places. *3-Shops serving center workers* provide goods and services to the workers of the CBD. Examples are copy stores, shoe repair, and computer stores. Business persons such as lawyers, financiers, journalists and advertisers are often clustered in the downtown for they are very interdependent. Locating firms together facilitates meetings between the various professionals. Central locations also allow employees to choose between a variety of housing and neighborhoods, all reasonably accessible to the city center.

Consequences of High Land Costs in the CBD (523-525): Because land is very desirable in the CBD's and its area is relatively small, property prices in downtown areas are exorbitant. Tokyo's land prices are the highest in the world, as high as $250,000 per square meter. Prices are inflated by a shortage of buildable land. The intense demand for land in CBD's has caused people to utilize spaces both below and above the ground's surface. Under the ground exist subways, parking garages, and utility lines. Toronto and Minneapolis have created subsurface corridors for shopping areas. Skyscrapers have been built in the world's largest cities creating distinctive urban skylines. The first skyscrapers were built in Chicago in the 1880's. Skyscrapers have caused traffic problems because they house large numbers of people, bringing many cars into small areas. Washington, DC doesn't have a high skyline like other cities of its size because zoning laws restrict the height of all buildings to no higher than the capitol building.

European CBD's (525): The structure of streets and buildings in European cities tend to be more irregular and smaller than in American cities. This is a legacy from medieval times. European cities have also tried to preserve the historical character of their cities; consequently, renovations are more common in European cities. Demand is even higher in European cities than in American urban areas and, logically, so are the rents.

Declining Activity in Central Cities (525-526): Manufacturing facilities today desire very large, one-story plots of land for industrial plans. Since CBD's tend to have expensive rents, many manufacturers have left for the cheaper real estate of the suburbs or outlying small towns. In response to the exodus of industries from city cores, city planners have often redesigned cities for recreation and retail shops. For example, formerly deteriorating waterfronts have been torn down and rebuilt with the tourist and suburbanite shopper in mind. CBD's have experienced an overall reduction in population because of associated poor social statistics of crime and poverty. Yet, in Europe people are more likely to live in CBD's. Many people in the U.S. must *commute* daily from the suburbs to the CBD, creating the rush hour—a time period when transportation areas are acutely crowded.

Inner City Housing (526-528): Most occupants of inner-cities in the U.S. are low-income African-Americans and Latinos. Often they will migrate to predominantly white areas, followed by many of the whites leaving to find more homogeneous areas to live. Large houses are often divided among poorer families. As time goes by the houses are neglected and eventually become abandoned because taxes exceed the income collected by the landlord. The process of home division and rental is known as *filtering*. *Blockbusting* is when real estate agents purchase homes cheaply from minority-threatened whites and then sell them to minorities for a considerable profit. *Redlining* is when banks delineate areas within the urban area to which they will not loan money because of high financial risk. *Urban renewal* was a practice which removed many city dwellers from blighted inner-city neighborhoods, selling the property to public agencies or private developers. It has become very unpopular and no longer receives funding from the U.S. government.

Public Housing and Inner City Elite(528-530): Much old, low-quality housing in the U.S. and Europe has been demolished and replaced by public housing. These units are reserved for low-income people who must pay a percentage of their income, such as thirty percent, for rent. In the U.S. only two percent of all housing is public, but in the United Kingdom it is over thirty percent of all housing in the country. Since the 1970's, funding from the

U.S. government for public housing units has nearly stopped. The government does subsidize some rents. Islands of wealthy people have maintained exquisite neighborhoods in the midst of the inner city. **Gentrification** occurs when people move back to the inner city to renovate homes. Nice architecture, inexpensive prices and access to the downtown draw many suburbanites back into the city.

Problems in Central Cities (530-532): With few exceptions, the inner city is home to people with social and economic problems. Due to high levels of crime, drug-addiction, illiteracy, and poor parental supervision of one-parent households, it is hard for inner city residents to occupationally and educationally progress in society. They are labeled the permanent **underclass**. Good learning habits are not practiced by many of the residents in their younger years, keeping them from elevating from low socio-economic levels. The **homeless**, people with no permanent housing, are now a fixture of the inner city environment. Sadly, many of these people have been released from hospitals and institutions and fail to cope with the modern world. Whites and blacks are generally segregated; Blacks tend to dwell in the inner cities while whites are found more often in the suburbs. Latino Americans tend to live in central cities. Many of the higher paid people have left the problem-strewn inner cities for the suburbs, devastating the tax-base of central cities and creating tight fiscal budgets which meant cut-backs in many public services.

Attraction of Suburbs (532-535): Opinion polls in the U.S. and Europe show that over ninety percent of people prefer to live in the suburbs. Families with children are especially attracted to suburbs because there is more green space and the schools tend to be far better than inner city schools. In the U.S., suburbs have grown much faster than the overall population from 1950 to the present. The housing density and lots upon which houses sit become larger further from the city core. This density change is called the **density gradient**. Europeans have used zoning laws to make density gradients flatter, or more uniform. **Sprawl** is the spread of development across the landscape. Suburbs often exist on former farmlands. Mandatory open spaces often encircle cities in Great Britain and are called **greenbelts**. Laws that prevent mixed land use such as commercial and residential overlapping property are called **zoning ordinances**. U.S. suburbs are criticized because poor people, often minorities, can not afford to live in them because housing prices are kept uniformly high. In 1954, the U.S. Supreme Court ruled that segregation is unconstitutional. Afterwards, many white and black students were bussed to schools in areas outside their neighborhoods to promote integration. Many white parents reacted to this by enrolling their students in private schools.

The Automobile (535-537): Because of urban sprawl, people have become more dependent on automated transportation. Before the automobile, people lived in dense cities with no option for living in suburbs because similar transportation simply did not exist. The automobile is responsible for 95 percent of all trips within U.S. cities. Highways paid for by the U.S. government have helped encourage the purchase of automobiles by the U.S. population. The average city allocates one-fourth of its land area to roads and parking lots. The implementation of new highways has caused disruptions in many older world cities where they are not easily placed.

Public Transit (537-538): Automobiles are very expensive to own and operate. Popularity must stem from convenience and privacy because public transportation is cheaper, less-polluting and more energy-efficient. Commitment to the automobile decreased the number of people using public transportation in the last fifty years. Public transportation use declined from 23 billion per year in the late 1940's to 7 billion per year in the early 1990's. New interest has developed in rapid transit lines. Funds earmarked for highways have recently been invested in the expansion of rapid transit systems. California leads in the construction of new light rail systems. Reduced subsidies to rapid transit lines threaten their existence. Unlike the U.S., Western European countries and Japan maintain and expand rapid transit because it is perceived as an important and desirable amenity.

Suburbanization of Retailing (538-542): Because richer and larger consumer bases are more frequently found in the suburbs, firms have located shopping malls in them. **Shopping malls** are elaborate, multilevel structures which house many retail establishments. They are frequently at road intersections and occupy more than 100 acres of land. A **developer** buys the land and constructs the mall, centering it around an anchor. An anchor is a large discount store or supermarket which attracts consumers who then frequent other shops in the mall. CBD's increasingly compete with retail centers found on the city's periphery. Sometimes they block streets off to all but pedestrian traffic which creates an outdoor-like atmosphere. Malls are also placed in downtown areas. As with retailing, many factories and offices have moved to the suburbs because of low-rents, availability of parking, and more space.

Three Models of Urban Structure (542-544): Sociologists, economists, and geographers have developed three models to depict the locations of where people live in urban areas. The **concentric zone model** was the first to describe social structures of areas surrounding CBD's. It was developed by **E. W. Burgess** in 1923, and postulated that a city grows outward from a CBD. The second ring is in transition between industry and poor housing. Stable, working class families occupy the third ring. Newer, more spacious homes occupy the fourth ring. Finally, the fifth ring includes small villages and bedroom communities populated by commuters. **Homer Hoyt** designed the **sector model**, which says cities develop in a series of sectors, not rings. He believed that activities evolved in a wedge shape with the most narrow tip being the CBD. The model is, to some extent, a refinement of the concentric zone model. Interestingly, both used the layout of Chicago to support the different models. **C. D. Harris and E. L. Ullman** developed the **multiple nuclei model** stating a city is a complex place in which different nodes develop. Nodes may be represented by parks, universities, ports, or business centers. Different types of nodes tend to attract certain types of people to them depending on offered services.

Geographic Applications of Models In U.S. Cities (544-547): In order to understand and digest the data concerning people's locations, the U.S. Census gathers information by **census tracts**, neighborhood areas each containing about 5,000 people. Demographic information is collected which can be analyzed. This type of study is called *social area analysis*. Models help describe spatial attributes of race, income, and transportation needs which contribute to better strategic decisions made by public and private sector institutions.

European and LDC Cities (547-554): Europe's wealthy tend to live in the inner cities while poor people, often immigrants, are relegated to dense public housing structures in the suburbs. European officials endorse building high density suburban housing so the countryside will be preserved from development. By living in the central part of the large metropolitan areas, Europe's upper classes have access to the best shops, historical places, and restaurants. However, due to the congestion which prevails, they must share green spaces (public parks). Some urban people purchase country homes to gain more private space which they may visit on weekends or holidays. The rich people in LDC's also reside in the city cores of their respective countries. Again, the poor are located in the more remote suburbs. During pre-colonial times, cities were formed around a religious core, such as a church or mosque. Businesses were placed in rings in which distance from the center depended on the business's perceived hierarchical value. Modern cities were planned. Wider streets, grid street plans, and open spaces were ways in which Europeans improved cities. In Latin America *Griffin* and *Ford* show the elite often settle along spines of development that contain restaurants, theaters, and other amenities attractive to richer people.

Squatter Settlements (554-555): LDC's are not able to provide housing for all residents. Many desire to live in the cities and are forced to dwell in shanty towns which occupy the fringes of many cities in Latin America, Africa, and Asia. Squatter settlements are known as barrios, favelas, bustees, and bidonvilles in different parts of the world. *Squatter settlements* initially begin as camp grounds where new immigrants live. Often, over long periods of time, they improve somewhat in structure. Sadly, many cities in the world have significant portions of their populations living in squatter settlements.

CLOSING REMARKS

The U.S. economy has shifted from primarily agriculture to manufacturing and finally to the service sector which signifies contemporary economies in MDC's. Along with changes in the economic base as well as the infusion of different technologies, the cities in which humans live have adjusted to the shift. In the U.S., most upper class people prefer to live in the suburbs which are increasingly attractive for industries. Europe's elite often live in the central cities of their urban complexes with poorer classes living in densely populated suburbs. Although planners may wish to create a more egalitarian living structure through planning, prices dictated by taxes, supply and demand prohibit such an urban structure from existing.

KEY TERMS AND CONCEPTS

Central Business District (CBD): The area of the city where retail and office activities are clustered. In large cities, the suburbs are often drawing CBD businesses away from the city center.

Rush Hour (peak hour): The four consecutive fifteen-minute periods in the morning and evening with the heaviest volumes of traffic. The suburbs have less congestion than the CBD's of most cities.

Filtering: A process of change in the use of a house, from single-family owner and occupancy to abandonment. The house costs eventually exceeds its income.

Blockbusting: A process by which real estate agents convince white property owners to sell their houses at low prices because of fear that nonwhite families will soon move into the neighborhood. Afterward, the houses are sold for large profits to minorities.

Redlining: A process by which banks draw lines on a map and refuse to lend money to purchase or improve property within the boundaries. Such properties are deemed as high financial risks by the banks.

Urban Renewal: A process where cities identified undesirable inner-city neighborhoods, relocated the occupants, cleared the site, and developed the land privately or publicly.

Public Housing: Housing owned by the government. In the United States, it is rented to low-income residents, and the rents are generally set at 30 percent of the families' incomes. Public housing in the U.S. has declined in recent years.

Gentrification: A process of converting an urban neighborhood from a predominantly low-income renter to a predominantly middle-class owner-occupied area. Classic architecture and low-prices are two things that encourage gentrification by the middle-class.

Underclass: A group in society prevented from participating in the material benefits of a more developed society because of a variety of social and economic characteristics. Poor education and high crime rates are often prevalent in such groups.

Density Gradient: The change in density in an urban area from the center to the periphery. As one moves outward from the city core, densities in the U.S. tend to decline.

Sprawl: Development of new housing sites at relatively low density and at locations that are not contiguous to the existing built-up area.

Greenbelts: A ring of land maintained as parks, agriculture, or other types of open space to limit the sprawl of an urban area. They have driven up housing prices in Europe.

Zoning Ordinances: A law limiting the permitted uses of land and maximum density of development in a community. These statutes attempt to prevent the mixing of land uses in neighborhoods.

Concentric Zone Model: A model of the internal structure of cities in which social groups are spatially arranged in a series of rings. E. W. Burgess developed it in 1923.

Sector Model: A model of the internal structure of cities in which social groups are arranged around a series of sectors or wedges radiating out from the CBD. Homer Hoyt developed this model in 1939.

Multiple Nuclei Model: A model of the internal structure of cities in which social groups are arranged around a collection of nodes of activities. E. L. Ullman and C. D. Harris developed this model in 1945.

Census Tracts: An area delineated by the U.S. Bureau of the Census for which statistics are published. In urbanized areas, census tracts correspond roughly to neighborhoods.

Edge City: A large node of office and retail activities on the edge of an urban area. Their lucrative traits are cheaper rents and room for expansion.

Squatter Settlements: An area within a city in a less developed country in which people illegally establish residences on land they do not own or rent and erect home-made structures. Rio de Janeiro, Brazil has extensive squatter settlements which are known as favelas.

1. CBD stands for a city's _____ _____ _____.   central business district

2. Stores needing a large customer base are said to be _____   high
threshold businesses.

3. The city of _____ is acknowledged to have the highest land   Tokyo
prices of any urban area on Earth.

4. High-rise structures which symbolize the American
metropolitan area's downtown are called _____.   skyscrapers

5. The first skyscrapers in the U.S. are found in the city of _____.   Chicago

6. The city of _____, _____ has no buildings higher than thirteen   Washington, DC
stories, the level of the U.S. Capitol's dome.

7. The renovation of older buildings is more prevalent in _____,   Europe
than in the U.S..

8. Many Europeans prefer to live in CBD's but Americans prefer
the _____ of their urban places.   suburbs

9. The daily traverse from the suburbs to the CBD by workers in
their automobiles is known as _____.   commuting

10. The time of heaviest traffic in a day is called the _____ hour.   rush

11. The subdivision of houses and consequent occupancy by
lower income people is known as _____.   filtering

12. _____ is the process by which banks refuse to lend money for   Redlining
houses situated in specific geographical areas.

13. Most North American and European cities have turned away
from urban _____ since the 1970's.   renewal

14. When older housing in the inner city is purchased and
renovated by younger, higher income people, _____ occurs.   gentrification

15. Inner-city residents who seem trapped in their low-income social group are called the permanent _____.

underclass

16. People who have no permanent housing and no income are called _____.

homeless

17. _____ transpires when people of different races and ethnicity live distinctly apart from one another.

Segregation

18. _____-Americans comprise over two-thirds of the populations of Atlanta, Detroit, and Washington, DC.

African

19. Over _____ percent of Americans polled prefer to live in the suburbs.

90

20. As one leaves the central city, the population density in U.S. cities usually _____.

declines

21. Progressive urban spread over the landscape is _____.

sprawl

22. Rings of parks around British cities are called _____.

greenbelts

23. Laws, in the form of _____ _____, encourage spatial separation.

zoning ordinances

24. Many _____-_____ and _____ people can not afford to move into suburban housing in the U.S..

low- income, minority

25. The invention of the _____ significantly reduced the percentage of people who used public transportation in the U.S. during the twentieth century.

automobile

26. The average U.S. city allocates one-fourth of its area to parking lots and _____.

roads

27. Elaborate, multiple-level _____ _____ are located in the suburbs where their consumers tend to live.

shopping malls

28. The observation developed by Homer Hoyt which explained the spatial array of economic activities in urban areas is called the _____ _____.

Sector Model

29. E. L. Ullman helped develop the _____ _____ model that said different urban activities are clustered near nodes.

Multiple Nuclei

30. In Europe, suburbs often have _____ crime rates than do   higher
cities.

31. _____ _____ are known as favelas in _____.   Squatter settlements, Brazil

CHAPTER THIRTEEN

RESOURCE PROBLEMS

OVERVIEW

Humans make many choices about the world around them. They must decide everything from what to make the house out of, to how to get to work. As economies have grown more complex, industry and manufacturing have risen to the challenge of providing everything wanted: televisions, automobiles, fertilizers, paints, and wrist watches. There is a negative side, too. Cars produce air pollution. Fertilizers contribute to water pollution. Disposal of paints contributes to soil pollution. By-products (heat, light, chemicals, acids, toxins, and sludge) are produced for everything manufactured and consumed. With more people comes more wants. More wants mean more consumption. More consumption means more pollution. Taking care of the Earth is perhaps one of the greatest challenges for not just the twenty-first century, but also for today.

SELECTED NOTES

Pollution in Mexico City (564): Mexico City is an example of extreme urban pollution. Among its worst forms of pollution is its poor air quality. The elevation of Mexico City at 7,400 feet makes the air thin, but added to this are pollutants from automobiles, factories, refineries, and other sources, which are constantly compacted against the valley walls which form the perimeter of the city on all but one side. Winds from the open north side of the valley compact the pollutants against the other three sides of the valley, causing very unhealthy smog. Most of the emissions in the air come from automobiles. Factories add to emitted pollutants. The Mexican government has restricted car use and has closed some industrial facilities to lower to the toxicity of the air in their capital. Sewage flows openly into nearby rivers, and 30 percent of the city's homes have no connections to the public sewer system.

Resource Brief (565): Humans frequently do not live harmoniously with nature. Invariably, resources are not utilized properly by humans; waste and pollution are the consequences. Geographers say that humans misuse resources in the following ways: *1-Depletion of scarce resources, 2-Destruction of resources through pollution,* and *3-Inefficient use of resources.* The study of resource management as a planet is probably the best use of globalization; resources extend across the Earth.

Fossil Fuels (565-567): The use of power by humans or animals is named *animate energy.* Power from machines is called *inanimate energy* is the result. *Oil, natural gas, and coal* provide over ninety percent of the energy in the U.S.. Historically, *biomass* (wood, plant material, and animal waste) has been and continues to be a very important source of energy It is burned directly or converted into methane gas, charcoal, or alcohol. Energy is important to businesses, homes, and transportation. A *fossil fuel* is the residue of plants and animals buried for millions of years. Fossil fuels are finite; they are limited in supply. They are unevenly distributed throughout the world. *Renewable* energy is limitless in amounts such as wind, solar, fusion, and hydroelectric. *Nonrenewable* energy can only be used once and will not be replaced within the life of a human being. Fossil fuels and fission nuclear energy are nonrenewable sources of energy. A *proven reserve* is the remaining amount of a nonrenewable resource. Reserves that are thought, but not proven, to exist are called its *potential reserve*. At current consumption rates the Earth's oil reserves will last another forty years. Coal is plentiful compared to oil and natural gas.

Extraction of Remaining Reserves (567-568): As time passes, the extraction of fossil fuels will become more difficult and costly. Coal mined today comes from seams which are relatively poor in quality compared to those mined in the past. The future will see the refinement of *oil shales* (rocks saturated with oil) and *tar sands* (oil-saturated sand). It is currently not profitable to process these energy sources as cost-effective technology has yet to be developed.

Uneven Distribution of Fossil Fuels (568-570): *Fossil fuels* were formed from tropical swamps which, because of tectonic movement, migrated poleward producing oil, coal, and natural gas. The U.S. and Russia each have a quarter of the world's reserves of coal. Europe has about twenty percent and China ten percent. Most of the world's oil supply is found in Saudi Arabia (25 percent) and other countries located near the Persian Gulf (40 percent). Countries such as Russia, Turkmenistan, and Uzbekistan possess one-third of the world's reserves of natural gas. Most places in Africa, Latin America, and other parts of Asia are relatively fossil fuel poor. Today a handful of countries consume seventy-five percent of the world's energy. As LDC's increase their economic status, they will place an even greater demand upon the reserves of fossil fuels in the world.

Control of World Petroleum (570-573): MDC's import most of their petroleum from the Middle East. Many of the reserves were controlled by Western European and U.S. oil companies until the 1950's when operations were largely monopolized. To reduce competition that drove down oil prices, a cartel was formed to set high prices for the MDC customers. This cartel is known as OPEC, Organization of Petroleum Exporting Countries, and has used its influence to increase the cost of oil. In 1973, these countries caused an energy crisis in the West when they boycotted oil exports as a form of protest for Western countries aiding Israel in the 1973 Arab-Israeli War. OPEC's effectiveness has been reduced in the last two decades because of many disputes between member countries. After the Persian Gulf war between the U.S., Kuwait, and Iraq the price of oil fell after briefly rising at the onset of the war to over forty dollars per barrel.

Problems With Coal (573-575): Coal is a resource for which large reserves exist, enough to serve U.S. needs for hundreds of years. Air pollution is caused when coal is burned, releasing sulfur oxides, hydrocarbons, and carbon dioxides. Scrubbers are placed on smoke stacks to minimize the amount of pollution emitted into the air. In the past thousands of miners perished annually in accidents; today the annual number of deaths is below 100. Coal mines cause land to subside and to erode easier. Water is often acidified after exposure to coal mines. Coal is costly to transport for it is bulky and heavy. Electric cars are ultimately powered by the coal burned to produce the electricity.

Nuclear Energy (575-578): Large amounts of energy are produced by small amounts of material when nuclear energy is produced through fission. Western Europe is largely powered by nuclear facilities. The U.S. produces about 20 percent of its electricity by nuclear energy. *Fission* is the splitting of atoms producing nuclear reactions that heat water, turn turbines and result in electricity. Another result is *toxic waste,* which can be deadly if humans are exposed to it. Nuclear waste does not lose its radioactivity for thousands of years, hence permanent storage facilities are difficult to find. Reactions may runaway, causing a *meltdown* as happened at Chernobyl in the Soviet Union, killing 31 people. Uranium also has a limited supply, only about sixty more years at current levels of use. A *breeder reactor* turns uranium into plutonium as a renewable resource. But plutonium is far more lethal and may be more easily placed into nuclear bombs. Nuclear plants are also extremely expensive to build and maintain. *Costs and risks* are the main impediments to more nuclear facilities.

Solar Energy (578-579): Solar energy is free and will be present for about 5 billion years. *Passive solar energy systems* collect energy without special devices such as human skin or dark clothing. *Active solar energy systems* collect solar energy and convert it either to heat energy or electricity. Heat conversion uses mirrors to reflect sunlight into lenses that heat water or rocks. *Indirect electric conversion* heats oil, running turbines on steam. *Direct electric conversion* uses *photovoltaic cells* to convert light energy directly into electricity. Solar energy is very popular in the U.S., Israel, and Japan.

Other Energy Sources (579-580): Water may be used to turn turbines as it falls, causing electricity. This is called *hydroelectric power*. This is the world's second most common form of electricity after coal. Dams are sometimes built which flood land and upset ecosystems, making hydroelectric plants less desirable. *Geothermal energy* is naturally occurring hot water heated by underground forces. It is found in active volcanic regions of the world. *Biomass* in the form of sugar cane, corn and soybeans may be processed into motor vehicle fuels. Biomass will likely not be increased as a source of fuel because it is already fulfilling many other human demands. *Fusion* is a potentially limitless source of energy, but temperatures created by such reactions can not yet be controlled.

Air Pollution (580-585): *Air pollution* is the concentration of trace substances at a level greater than that which occurs in average air. Carbon monoxide, sulfur dioxides, and nitrogen oxides are common pollutants of air. Cars, industry, and power plants cause most of the air pollution in the world. On a global scale human pollution of the Earth's air may be causing the temperature of the Earth to rise. Earth's surface temperatures have increased by one degree Celsius during the last 100 years. Many people attribute the rise in temperature to the *greenhouse effect*. If temperatures rise significantly more, the ice caps could melt and climate patterns around the planet would be disrupted. The *ozone* is a layer of air within the stratosphere which absorbs much of the ultra-violet rays from the sun. CFC's produced by people have damaged this zone, causing higher surface levels of UV exposure than in the past. *Acid precipitation* is produced when industry emits sulfur and nitrogen oxides into the atmosphere. *Acid deposition* damages water bodies and biomass. In the U.S., acid deposition originates in the highly industrialized areas around the Great Lakes. Eastern Europe has also suffered environmental damage because of acid rain and deposition. On local levels, carbon monoxide causes much biological damage to humans as it reduces oxygen in the blood when inhaled. Hydrocarbons and nitrogen oxides can form photochemical smog when released into the atmosphere, causing respiratory problems in exposed people. *Denver* has the worst air in the U.S. according to the EPA. Many LDC cities such as Santiago, Chile experience very intense air pollution. Air is becoming cleaner in MDC's where legislation is enforced. In countries where the population is beginning to drive, more air pollution grows accordingly.

Water Pollution (585-587): Water is imperative to human survival, yet it is frequently polluted by humans. Pollution of waterways is widespread. Rivers, lakes, and the ocean are very accessible to humans. Industries pollute waterways used as part of the industrial process in manufacturing or in chemical production. Municipal sewage pollutes water because it is difficult to extract all of the pollutants in the treatment stage. Fertilizers and pesticides runoff from watersheds to concentrate in streams and lakes, causing damage to the aquatic ecosystems. Nonpoint polluters are hard to stop, for their area of pollution is large and unfocused. Biochemical oxygen demand occurs when oxygen is consumed by organic waste, depleting the amount of oxygen that may be utilized by animal life in the water system. In MDC's today, diseases caused or carried by polluted water are relatively rare. Yet, in LDC's such diseases are common because of the lack of good water treatment facilities in urban areas.

Land Pollution (587-591): Products consumption results in solid waste that is incinerated, put into a dump, or recycled. *Sanitary landfills* are the most common disposal for solid waste in the U.S.. Solid wastes are concentrated into small areas of land, possibly affecting ground water supplies. They also drive down land prices. Consequently, many urban areas export waste to poorer parts of the country where disposal is overlooked because of financial gains. *Incineration* burns solid waste. This can be helpful when energy is derived from such burning. Sometimes toxins are released into the atmosphere during this process. *Recycling* solid waste prevents it from being placed in a landfill or incinerated. Many U.S. communities have forced people to recycle certain products. Recycling has increased to 22 percent of all solid waste in 1994. Toxic wastes found in heavy metals are harder to dispose of than other materials. People fear being near toxic waste sites because they can be very harmful. Many toxic substances are known to cause health problems in the human body even in small concentrations. This was the case at *Love Canal,* New York. Some U.S. and European firms have exported toxic wastes to West Africa to avoid government and public scrutiny at home.

Reducing Pollution By Reducing Discharges (591-592): If the amount of residue created is reduced, so may be pollution. Decreasing the number and amount of inputs into a product will decrease the amount of pollution the product creates. If demand for a product is reduced, so will the pollution caused by such a product. Recycling will also lower the number of inputs placed into a product. Using waste for a different or alternative use will make manufacturing more efficient, reducing pollution.

Increasing Environmental Capacity (592-596): Increasing the ability of the environment to absorb pollution also reduces the stress caused by pollution. This can be done by increasing the efficiency of the resources currently receiving discharges. For example, smokestacks can be built in areas with high winds to disperse and weaken pollutants. Residues can also be transformed and then expelled into other parts of the environment. For example, scrubbers are placed into the smokestacks of plants to make them more efficient.

Increasing the Food Supply (596-598): Agricultural production can be increased without negative effects. Restrictions can be placed on the amount of land consumed each year by urban sprawl. Housing is often built on premium farm land. Most scientists believe that shortages in world food supplies will not be compensated for employing these measures. Desertification is constantly reducing the amount of farmable land. The best way to increase food production is through research to develop more efficient genetic varieties of crops like wheat and rice. The green revolution of the 1970's and 1980's greatly increased world food production through these techniques. Wheat varieties were developed which were better suited to harsh environments and matured quicker than other types. This created substantially increased harvests of wheat. Fertilizers that inject nitrogen into the ground are another way to increase yields. This re-energizes the ground after crops tire it. Current fertilizers are often derived from oil bases. If oil prices go up, it becomes harder to fertilize crops, and yields drop accordingly.

New Food Supplies(598-600): The oceans can probably supply a much larger percentage of our food. The oceans are vast, covering three-fourths of the Earth's surface. If fishing is kept efficient, preventing overfishing, harvests from the sea can consistently be very large. Since much of the world doesn't consume very much animal protein, it is important to develop cereal grains that have high protein contents. If varieties of corn and wheat had higher levels of protein, many people in LDC's would maintain better health. Improving the variety of goods consumed improves diet and health. Americans would be healthier if soybeans were part of the daily diet. More balanced crop exports to needier places on the planet would alleviate pressure to grow large amounts of food in places which are naturally agriculturally disadvantaged. The U.S. could export crops and surpluses to African countries.

Africa's Food Supply Crisis (600-601): Sub-Saharan Africa cannot produce enough food for its population. It is estimated that 70 percent of Africans do not have enough food to eat. Agricultural production today is lower than it was in the 1950's. Farmers overplanted, land was overgrazed, and the soil was exhausted. Today, government conflicts add to the crises which plague African nations and threaten their survival.

CLOSING REMARKS

In the ultimate analysis, the resources available to humans (and how they use those resources) will determine the human geography of the future. The twentieth century will be remembered as the century in which most natural petroleum resources were consumed. Almost certainly the twenty-first century will see an increase in per capita use of resources, but without petroleum resources to provide the base like it did during the twentieth century. Coal will be available, but its threat to the environment may render it useless. Alternate energy sources will be exploited. Chapter thirteen lays a good foundation to understand what might happen and where, as a capstone for the body of human geography provided by the previous twelve chapters.

KEY TERMS AND CONCEPTS

Resource: A substance in the environment useful to people, and economically and technologically feasible to access, and socially acceptable to use.

Animate Power: Power supplied by people or animals. Today, it is used more in LDC's than in MDC's.

Inanimate Power: Power supplied by machines. This type of power dominates today's automated world.

Fossil Fuel: Energy source formed from the residue of plants and animals buried millions of years ago. They will be gone within 100 years, except coal, if used at current rates of consumption.

Renewable Energy: A resource that has a theoretically unlimited supply and is not depleted when used by people. Sunlight is an example.

Nonrenewable Energy: A source of energy that has a finite supply. Oil and natural gas are examples.

Proven Reserve: The amount of a resource remaining in discovered deposits. China and Russia are not open about their reserves.

Potential Reserve: The amount of energy in deposits not yet identified but thought to exist.

Air Pollution: Concentration of trace substances, such as carbon monoxide, sulfur dioxide, nitrogen oxides, hydrocarbons, and solid particles, at a greater level than occurs in average air.

Fission: The splitting of an atomic nucleus to release energy. It is the common technique used to create nuclear energy.

Fusion: The creation of energy by joining the nuclei of two hydrogen atoms to form helium. It produces heat which can not be contained by modern laboratories.

Radioactive Waste: Particles from a nuclear reaction that emit radiation. Contact with such particles may be harmful or lethal to people and must therefore be safely stored for thousands of years.

Breeder Reactor: A nuclear power plant that creates its own fuel from plutonium. They are more dangerous than other reactors and are not found in the U.S..

Passive Solar Energy Systems: Solar energy system that collects energy without the use of mechanical devices. Animal skin and dark clothing are examples.

Active Solar Energy Systems: Solar energy system that collects energy through the use of mechanical devices like photovoltaic cells or flat-plate collectors. Solar cells on roofs are examples.

Photovoltaic Cells: Solar energy cells, usually made from silicon, that collect solar rays to generate electricity. Enough cells can propel small cars.

Hydroelectric Power: Power generated from moving water. There is little future opportunity for this power in the U.S. because most of the good sites are already being used.

Geothermal Energy: Energy from steam or hot water produced from hot or molten underground rocks. In the U.S., Yellowstone National Park has good geothermal energy potential.

Biomass: Fuel derived from plant material and animal waste. Animal wastes can be "fermented" to produce methane gas, used in some areas where wood fuel is difficult or impossible to obtain.

Pollution: Addition of more waste than a resource can accommodate. It often decreases the value of other natural resources.

Greenhouse Effect: Anticipated increase in Earth's temperature, caused by carbon dioxide (emitted by burning fossil fuels) trapping some of the radiation emitted by the surface. The melting of the polar ice-caps could be a long-term result of this phenomena.

Ozone: A gas which absorbs ultraviolet solar radiation, found in the stratosphere, a zone between 15 and 50 kilometers above Earth's surface. It is widely thought that it is being depleted by chemical reactions.

Chlorofluorocarbon (CFC): A gas used as a solvent, a propellant in aerosols, a refrigerant, in plastic foams and fire extinguishers. Its presence is thought to be destroying the ozone.

Acid Deposition: Sulfur oxides and nitrogen oxides, emitted by burning fossil fuels, enter the atmosphere where they combine with oxygen and water to form sulfuric acid and nitric acid and return to Earth's surface. Here they destroy many botanical surface features of the Earth.

Acid Precipitation: Conversion of sulfur oxides and nitrogen oxides to acids that return to Earth as rain, snow, or fog. They cause bodies of water to become acidified.

Photochemical Smog: An atmospheric condition formed through a combination of weather conditions and pollution, especially from motor vehicle emissions. Denver has the worst in the U.S..

Biochemical Oxygen Demand (BOD): Amount of oxygen required by aquatic bacteria to decompose a given load of organic waste, a measure of water pollution.

Sanitary Landfill: A place to dispose solid waste, where a layer of Earth is bulldozed over garbage each day to reduce emissions of gases and odors from the decaying trash, minimize fires, and discourage vermin. It is difficult to open new ones because of public resistance.

Desertification: Degradation of land, especially in semiarid areas, primarily due to human actions like excessive crop planting, animal grazing, and tree cutting. Substantial desertification has occurred in Africa.

Green Revolution: Rapid diffusion of new agricultural technology, especially new high-yield seeds and fertilizers. Wheat and rice crops have increased substantially.

Sustainable Development: The level of development that can be maintained in a country without depleting resources to the extent that future generations will be unable to achieve a comparable level of development.

CHAPTER THIRTEEN   <u>Progressive Review</u>

1. Mexico City suffers from extreme _____ pollution.   air

2. Animal and human power is also known as _____ power.   animate

3. Energy is used heavily in businesses, homes, and _____.   transportation

4. Coal is an example of _____ energy.   nonrenewable

5. Sunlight is an example of _____ energy.   renewable

6. Mineral deposits that are known to exist are called _____ _____.   proven reserves

7. Mineral deposits which are thought to exist are known as _____ _____.   potential reserves

8. _____ sands and oil _____ are rocks and stone which are oil-saturated.   Tar, shales

9. At current rates of consumption the world's oil supply will dry up in _____ years.   40

10. _____ supplies will last much longer than oil and natural gas.   Coal

11. The base for coal was formed millions of years ago in tropical _____.   swamps

12. MDC's tend to have a _____ percentage of the world's fossil fuels.   high

13. Two-thirds of the world's oil reserves are found in the _____ _____.   Middle East

14. OPEC largely controls the world's supply of _____.   oil

15. After the _____-_____ war, OPEC boycotted oil exports to the West.   Arab-Israeli

16. The South American country of _____ is a member of OPEC.   Venezuela

17. Annual mortality rates in _____ is now less than 100 annually.   mining

18. _____ is more difficult to transport than other fossil fuels.   Coal

19. _____ _____ produces a large amount of energy from a small amount of material.   Nuclear energy

20. The splitting of an atom in a nuclear reaction is called _____.   fission

21. The two primary radioactive materials used for nuclear reactions are _____ and _____.   uranium, plutonium

22. Power derived from moving water is called _____ electricity.   hydro

23. Geothermal forces heat _____ into steam which then runs turbines.   water

24. Atoms are combined in the process of _____.   fusion

25. Anticipated warming of the Earth is part of the _____ effect.   greenhouse

26. CFC's are thought to be destroying the _____ layer in the atmosphere.   ozone

27. Most solid waste in the U.S. goes into _____ _____.   sanitary landfills

28. _____ reduces solid waste to 25 percent its original size.   Incineration

29. When land is overgrazed and deteriorates to a point where it cannot be used it experiences _____.   desertification

30. Genetic improvements made on plants which increase harvests are collectively referred to as the _____ _____.   green revolution